W9-DBC-522

Screaming Eagle

Screaming Eagle
Memoirs of a B-17 Group Commander

By Dale O. Smith
Major General, U.S. Air Force (Ret.)

Algonquin Books of Chapel Hill
1990

Published by
Algonquin Books of Chapel Hill
Post Office Box 2225
Chapel Hill, North Carolina 27515-2225

a division of
Workman Publishing Company, Inc.
708 Broadway
New York, New York 10003

Library of Congress Cataloging-in-Publication Data
Smith, Dale O.
  Screaming eagle : memoirs of a B-17 group commander /
by Dale O. Smith.
    p. cm.
  ISBN 0-912697-99-7
  1. World War, 1939–1945—Aerial operations, American. 2. Smith,
Dale O. 3. World War, 1939–1945—Personal narratives, American.
4. United States. Army Air Forces. Bomb Group (H), 384th. 5. World War,
1939–1945—Campaigns—Germany. 6. Air pilots, Military—United
States—Biography. 7. United States—Armed Forces—History—World War,
1939–1945. I. Title.
D790.S568   1990
940.54′4973—dc20   89-18230
                                                           CIP

First edition
10 9 8 7 6 5 4 3 2 1

To my loyal and loving wife,
Virginia Posvar Smith

Contents

Illustrations

Acknowledgments

I am grateful to Louis D. Rubin, Jr., for his insightful advice and editing of my manuscript, and to my wife, Virginia, who has read, corrected, and commented on the whole manuscript many times over. I am also grateful to the editors of *Air Force, The Retired Officer,* and *Aerospace Historian* magazines for allowing me to use previously published material. Just before going to press I received a vivid narrative by Col. Anthony Palazzo on the role of a bombardier, and I have included it as an appendix. I am in his debt for allowing me to use this material. My thanks go to many other members of the 384th Bomb Group, Inc., who have helped me with this work.

Many thanks to personnel of the USAF Historical Research Center at Air University, Maxwell AFB, Alabama, for their help in finding many old records of the 384th. But *no* thanks to whomever in Hq. USAAF changed our prized insignia and cast in concrete an insignia we never saw and which now adorns the B-1B's of the present 384th.

Screaming Eagle

1
Premonitions

You might as well go to sleep, I told myself, because no matter how scared you get, you sure as hell *are* going on that B-17 mission over Germany tomorrow. I turned and tossed on a rock-hard British cot, trying to purge my mind of what seemed my almost certain demise. I had heard too many gory tales about the Eighth Air Force. Visions of a fiery death in a screaming dive tormented me.

Again and again I tried to reason with myself: You deliberately chose the profession of arms. You had no reservations when you took the oath on the Plain at West Point. You knew what the obligation was—that it might require the ultimate sacrifice. You took the Queen's Shilling, as they say. And now this is the payoff. You're not going to back down now. No. This is what it's all about. And you're a professional. A regular. If you're shot down tomorrow, so be it.

But sleep would not come. Over and over I argued with myself. I wasn't prepared to die. I was thirty-two years old, with a wife and two fine kids. Again and again Elise had pleaded with me not to take this assignment. She was well aware of the heavy losses the new U.S. Eighth Air Force was experiencing in Europe, and, having lost a brother on the Bataan death march, she didn't want to lose her husband, too. She couldn't understand why I felt I had to get into combat. To her I was simply being pigheaded. Tonight I began to think she had a point.

A wife and children at home? What a fatuous argument! How many thousands of others had loving wives and kids at home?

Nine years of military flying had not yet made me a fatalist. I regretted that I had been so gung ho as to get myself into this fix, when I could have remained in the States training others to go to war. When the AAF Antisubmarine Command was broken up, Gen. Swede Larson had been given command of a training air force with headquarters in Florida and he had asked me to go with him, hinting at a promotion to brigadier general. Why hadn't I taken him up on such a cushy offer?

Yet I didn't really regret my decision to join the Eighth Air Force. This was what I truly wanted to do. I had gained something of a reputation as a matériel officer while with the Antisub Command and could envision spending the war as a staff officer. I thought the Florida assignment would be the kiss of death, as far as my career was concerned. So it was with some relief that I had broken loose from that mold and was on my way for an operational combat command.

I wanted to fight with the Eighth in Europe, the big league of combat aviation. I wanted to share in the direct attack on Hitler's Fortress Europe. I had worked all kinds of angles to get here. Now I was about to go on my first combat mission with the Eighth—and, I thought, probably my last.

The loss rate in the Eighth Air Force in the fall of 1943 was something like 4 or 5 percent per mission. The cards seemed unfairly stacked in favor of extinction. And during that terrifying night I knew for sure that my luck had run out. It was a premonition, I told myself. Nevertheless, I *was* committed and I *would* fly.

My flying days up to now had not been without moments of terror. I had survived three crack-ups and lucked out on several hairy mishaps. But I had always held a lingering doubt. Did I possess the same cool courage that some of my contemporaries had demonstrated in moments of danger? What was their secret? Had they been born without fear?

One group commander in the Eighth Air Force had advised his crews to consider themselves dead already. Perhaps if one could do this there would be no fear, but I couldn't bring myself to accept such a final solution.

Bob Williams, a cool, friendly officer with a warm smile, had been my group commander at Langley Field two years earlier. There we had been assigned the very first B-17s, and I knew the airplane like the back of my hand. Hunting submarines had had its perils, but there hadn't been much shooting. The great battles of the Eighth Air Force over Europe—Saint-Nazaire, Schweinfurt, Regensburg, Villacoublay—were where the real action was. To me this air campaign seemed the most dangerous, if not the most important, in the whole American war effort at that time.

Bob Williams had lost an eye while observing the Battle of Britain in 1940, and when he looked at you his glass eye was focused elsewhere. But his voice was low and firm, and he was regarded as one of the most capable and experienced division commanders in the growing Eighth Air Force. I knew he would live up to his promise of giving me command of one of his groups, provided that I demonstrated an aggressive spirit. At that time each of his groups consisted of about thirty-six Flying Fortresses and crews, with supporting personnel of up to three thousand on one air station. Command of an air group was the prized goal of most flying colonels.

A week before that sleepless night I had reported to Bob, reminding him of his promise. He and his staff briefed me at length on the manifold problems I would encounter. Attrition of group commanders was high, and Bob had some vacancies. He offered me the unlucky and badly shot-up 384th Group located at Grafton Underwood, a tiny town near Kettering in North-ampton. Morale and discipline in that outfit, he told me, were so low that he had considered disbanding the group altogether and sending the crews to more successful outfits. With naive over-confidence I was convinced I could whip the 384th into shape. I had done it before with the 20th Bomb Squadron back home. A group composed of four squadrons would be just a little tougher job.

"First," Bob said, "I want you to spend some time with Willie Hatcher's group, the 351st. That's one of my best, and you can learn a lot from Willie." Bob didn't tell me to go on missions with the 351st, but I knew he expected me to. There was some talk around division headquarters about replacement group commanders needing to be "blooded." I didn't appreciate the term, but I realized what it meant. A group commander had to understand just what the cutting edge of a group was meant to do over enemy country, and he couldn't lead from a desk chair.

Finding my way to Polebrook in East Anglia, I had reported to the debonair Willie Hatcher, a superb leader and a friendly teacher. I followed him like a shadow, determined to learn all I could. Willie was always dressed for parade and he carried doeskin gloves. VIPs were frequently sent to Willie's group to see how the air war was being fought. Clark Gable had flown a few missions from that base as a gunner, and Lana Turner had visited to raise morale. Willie showed me the hallowed sleeping bag Lana had slept in and allowed me to smell the heady perfume that still lingered there. Willie's officers had a wild party one night and my brother, Thor, came up from London. Thor was on General Eisenhower's planning staff. After the party Thor and I sat on a bunk in a cold hut and talked and shivered almost all night. We both felt that it might be our last visit.

All of this was exciting and dramatic, but I knew the real war was in the air over Germany, and I asked Willie to schedule me for a mission. It turned out to be an attack on the port of Wilhelmshaven. The date was November 3, 1943.

I would have no responsibilities on the mission to Wilhelmshaven; I would just sandbag in the lead aircraft piloted by a veteran survivor of ten missions, Clint Ball. I could sit on a jump seat between the pilot and copilot or move around the aircraft to various positions, provided I didn't interfere with the duties of the crewmen. I chose to ride in the plexiglass nose, called the "greenhouse," for there I could man one of the three flexible .50-caliber machine guns sticking out of the nose. (The chin turret had not yet been incorporated into B-17 armament.) Neither the bombardier nor the navigator would have much time to shoot while they computed the track and bomb run.

It was good to leave that torturous bed where I had thrashed all night. I didn't feel a bit groggy for lack of sleep. If the gut fear hadn't kept me alert, the frigid air and icy floor of the Nissen hut did. A delicious breakfast in Willie's excellent mess did little to melt the hard rocks that seemed to have grown in my stomach.

The briefing that followed indicated the numerous enemy gun emplacements and Luftwaffe fighters we would likely encounter. It did little to alleviate my churning anxiety. I looked around at the sea of sober faces. How could I hope to command one of these magnificent groups when I was so deficient in courage? It wouldn't be fair to the brave men who were fighting the war so nobly and taking their chances without a whimper. Perhaps I should go to Bob Williams and tell him honestly that I just didn't have the guts to lead a combat group. Yes, that's what I'd do. But not until after this mission to Wilhelmshaven—if by chance I survived.

2

War Begins for the 20th

"**I** want the largest lobster in the house, and let me see it first—alive."

This was my dad ordering dinner at O'Donnell's, a famous seafood restaurant in Washington. I think he was trying to impress me, but there was no doubt about his voracious appetite for shellfish. He used to tell me with delight how fresh oysters, packed in ice, were hauled by wagon from Maryland to Nevada and sold in Virginia City for one dollar each. When he told me the story, one dollar was a wildly exorbitant price, even back home in Reno where I grew up.

It was December of 1941, and I had flown to Washington from Langley Field, Virginia, the week before to attend to some matters at the Munitions Building—the Pentagon had not yet been built—regarding my secret orders to Iceland. "Project Indigo" was the code name to launch the squadron I commanded, the 20th of the 2nd Bomb Group, into an undeclared war. The fact that Dad just happened to be in Washington on business had nothing to do with my trip, of course.

It was Sunday and I wanted to get back to Langley Field at a reasonable hour, so we were having an early dinner. Dad polished off every edible morsel of that huge crustacean, then he hailed a taxi and we drove through the tangled traffic to

Bolling Field, where my shiny new North American B-25 medium bomber was spotted on the apron in front of Operations.

I didn't know when I would see Dad again. Of course I couldn't tell him about my orders, but he seemed to sense that this visit had some hidden significance. He knew all about my squadron getting spanking new airplanes—something unusual in those days when we were sending everything to the embattled British.

As my copilot was working on the clearance to Langley Field I proudly showed Dad around my sleek two-engined bomber and he was duly impressed, although he didn't know enough about it to ask many questions. We were standing under a wing attempting to say good-bye, somewhat at a loss for words to express our profound regard and affection for each other, when my crew chief came running out from Operations.

"Major," he gasped, "the Japs have bombed Pearl Harbor! It's on the radio."

"That could be a spoof," I responded. We had been getting all kinds of wild rumors in those alarming days, even about an invasion from Mars. "Go back and check it out again."

There was an obvious stirring on the flight line and Dad knew something big was brewing. I told him a radio station had reported that the Japs had bombed Pearl Harbor. He didn't question the news for a moment. Then he accurately assessed the situation with the two words most Americans were using: "Those bastards!"

The crew chief came running back from Ops to say that the report was indeed authentic. All stations were carrying it. So the balloon had gone up. Even though I had expected it to happen sometime soon, the fact that we were now actually in an all-out war struck me with a visceral blow, because I knew I'd be in the thick of it, and I also knew how woefully unprepared was our Air Force.

I needed to get back to my squadron at once. I shook hands

with Dad as we looked deeply into each other's eyes and said a final goodbye. (In those days men didn't hug each other.) Then I climbed aboard and started the big radial engines, while Dad stood back and watched, motionless, until we taxied off.

As a regular officer, the imminence of war had loomed large in my thoughts. I agonized over the knowledge that America was deficient in almost everything that could lead to victory or even prevent defeat. Oh, I believed we'd win in the end, but before that happened we would lose some bloody battles.

Congress had renewed the military draft by the margin of one vote, but many of the new recruits had to drill with wooden guns. Aircraft factories were beginning to turn out more warplanes, but not for us. First they were built for the French, and then for the British, while we continued to train with antiquated flying equipment.

Radar, which had so recently been largely responsible for giving the Royal Air Force the edge in the Battle of Britain, thus saving England from an invasion, was almost unknown to us in the Air Corps. Some halting steps were being taken by the Army to experiment with air defense systems, but priority for this work was so low that progress was almost negative. After all, who could attack America, or even Hawaii, from the air? Our surface-oriented Army and Navy simply could not visualize such a possibility.

Now, at Pearl Harbor, we were reaping the whirlwind of our stubborn ignorance. Flying back to Langley in the gathering dusk I tuned the radio compass to a commercial station and heard the incredible reports of the surprise attack on Pearl. It seemed that Japanese aviation had done great harm to our Pacific Fleet. It was obvious from the news reports that Pearl Harbor had been a humiliating defeat. At least, I thought, the Air Corps would never again have to justify the effectiveness of military aviation to the Army and Navy, not to mention the American public and Congress, who had been so reluctant in giving us the flying equipment we desperately needed. But old attitudes die hard, as I was soon to learn.

Iceland! I could think of a lot of places I'd rather fight the war from. But my orders had presented some exciting prospects, and I wasn't too unhappy about them. It hadn't taken any prescience to sense that we would soon be in a declared war and I would be getting the jump on other outfits. My squadron had been given an unheard-of priority for personnel and equipment, which was heady stuff in those days. I hadn't been told what our objective might be in Iceland, and it hardly had crossed my mind that we might be hunting submarines, about which we knew nothing at all. Within days I had received a full complement of eighteen North American B-25s right off the production line. These modern bombers, with tricycle landing gear and huge engines, were the fastest in the skies—or so we thought.

My crews had begun to flesh out with good men, and we had unscrupulously robbed other outfits of top maintenance and supply people. Six years in the Army Air Corps had never before permitted me to experience a squadron with full Table of Organization personnel and equipment. They had all operated at about half strength. Now the famine was over.

All this was flooding across my mind as I switched from one radio station to another and heard the repeated breathless reports. Two hours on a southerly course brought us to the familiar runway lights of Langley and I sat the plane down.

My assumption was that our orders for Indigo would remain unchanged, and I called an immediate meeting of 20th personnel. "Don't panic," I warned them, "like the rest of the country seems about to do. We have our orders and I'll tell you where we're going just as soon as they let me. In the meantime, just keep on doing what you have been doing—getting the squadron ready to move overseas."

I failed to anticipate the extent of the shock and fear that gripped the nation. That night I was kept awake with one phone call after another, some from the Olympic eminence of the Munitions Building itself, where it seemed that our top military leaders were rushing about yelling and gnashing their teeth. It was well known in higher circles that my squadron was up to strength and ready to move. Apparently Indigo had been scrubbed, and several plans were being hatched to use the 20th otherwise in the new war. That suited me fine. As the reality of Pearl Harbor hit me, I wanted to help avenge this disgrace, and I thought I had the weapons to do it.

Sometime after midnight I received orders that seemed authentic enough and through proper channels, if somewhat bizarre. I was to move the 20th ASAP—as soon as possible—to Mitchel Field on Long Island to guard New York City—against the Vichy French fleet!

Anyone who had followed the war in the newspapers knew that the British had destroyed or severely damaged a sizable part of the French fleet after France had capitulated. The less-than-formidable armada still afloat had been last heard from in the harbor of Toulon. Yet Intelligence feared that what was left of the fleet, having somehow eluded detection by the British Navy, might now be steaming west to bombard American cities. After the Pearl Harbor disaster, I imagine, the brass was sort of touchy about the whereabouts of an enemy fleet.

"ASAP" meant early that morning as far as my squadron was concerned. We were ready. I tried to send messages to the commander of Mitchel Field through Signal Corps channels, requesting billeting and messing accommodations for 350, but no word got through. No doubt the Army had higher-priority traffic and Air Corps business was put on the back burner. I then tried Western Union and the telephone, with no more success. It seemed that everybody in America was trying to phone or wire someone, and all circuits were hopelessly jammed. There was no such thing as a military priority in existence. That would come later, as America learned more about war. So, early on the morning of the eighth my squadron prepared to take off for Mitchel, with no one there knowing we were coming.

I kissed my sleepy wife, Elise, good-bye. She was used to these kinds of separations, but war was in the air now and I could see the worry in her brown eyes. I didn't awaken the two little ones, who were sleeping soundly.

The spires of New York City rose above the mist that cold December morning as we flew toward Long Island and Mitchel Field. I looked right and left at the formations of my eighteen silver birds, knowing that we were making plenty of noise, and I was pleased to give the early risers on Manhattan Island a small taste of the war.

One after another my pilots landed sharply behind me, and we taxied up in line in front of Operations, awaiting instructions for parking. None came. I cut my engines, crawled out, and found the Operations Office. The commanding officer was there. Saluting, I presented myself, described the verbal orders I'd received, and apologized for my inability to get the message through to him.

This was Colonel Johnson (mercifully I have forgotten his first name), a hawk-faced, grey-haired officer well past his prime. He wore balloon pilot wings, and I suspected he had only a meager understanding of the winged Air Corps. "We don't have room for your squadron here," he told me, "and besides I have received no orders concerning your move." He dismissed me curtly.

His operations officer, who was more sympathetic, found parking places on the cluttered airfield for my B-25s, and I left with my hungry crews to find some breakfast. But breakfast hour was over at Mitchel Field; not a single mess hall was open. An appeal to Colonel Johnson was fruitless. We'd have to wait for the noon meal.

At that point my administrative orders were to come from the Army's Eastern Defense Command, headed by Gen. Hugh

A. Drum, one of those generals who thought the Air Corps was a pain in the ass. I called there, requesting that Colonel Johnson be sent orders for the temporary duty of the 20th at Mitchel. But General Drum's headquarters was in great confusion, and so far as I knew Colonel Johnson never did get orders to accept the 20th. We were squatters there, with a special train and truck convoy en route bringing the rest of the squadron from Langley Field.

I had been instructed to take operational orders from the Navy's Eastern Sea Frontier, located at 90 Church Street in New York City and commanded by the haughty Vice Adm. Adolphus Andrews. So I called there, too, and urged them to see that Colonel Johnson got the necessary orders. But that headquarters was also in a funk, no doubt bending heaven and earth to locate the imaginary Vichy French fleet.

We were provided no barracks, and it took much argument with Colonel Johnson to get even a hangar where cots could be set up. Some of my officers slept in chairs at the Officers' Club or on the floor. I wondered whether the good colonel thought the principal mission of Mitchel Field was to provide pleasant accommodations for his housekeeping troops.

In the midst of this confusion I received another change of orders. My air echelon was to take off immediately for Hamilton Field, California. Obviously we were on the way to the real war in the far Pacific!

Our clean B-25s were lined up on the taxiway with props ticking over when I was called by the tower controller: "Your mission has been scrubbed by the commanding general, Eastern Defense Command. Please taxi back to your parking spaces."

The next day Eastern Sea Frontier ordered us on an Atlantic Ocean sweep to search for the invading French fleet. We were to fly four hundred miles out from Long Island, on courses that the Navy had established. It was a dreary, overcast day. I loaded six birds with 100-pound bombs, the only ones available, and led the flight. With untried airplanes, and not being used to flying over water, I was a bit apprehensive. Four hundred miles out in the wintry Atlantic seemed awfully far from shore, and we carried no survival gear.

Ten miles out we echeloned right and spread out as far as we could, while still retaining visual contact with the airplanes to the left and right. This permitted us to sweep a stretch of ocean about fifty to one hundred miles wide, depending on the visibility. For about two hours we flew due east, then turned north for a half hour before heading back to base on a course of 250 degrees. Except for a few fishing boats, we found nothing but whitecaps. Definitely no Vichy French navy.

Darkness overtook us before we made landfall. An overcast blanked out the moon and stars. With no lights on the surface of the ocean I had never experienced such a stygian black night, and I drew a long sigh of relief when the lights of Long Island dimly appeared ahead. Fortunately our dead reckoning navigation had been good, for the radio beacon at Mitchel had been shut down.

The whole of Long Island was lit up like a Christmas tree. Where Mitchel Field was supposed to be located, however, there was a black hole. Not a single light globe burned there.

"Mitchel tower, this is Major Smith with six B-25s low on fuel. Turn on your runway lights."

"Sorry, Major Smith, but Mitchel is totally blacked out. Orders from the base commander."

I was flabbergasted. "But I can't land these airplanes without lights. My pilots aren't familiar with your runways."

"Sorry, Sir. We have strict orders to turn on no lights."

Fifteen miles to the northwest, La Guardia Airport lay in plain view, ablaze with thousands of lights like a jewel in the necklace of Long Island. "Take over and land the flight at La Guardia," I told my deputy, 1st Lt. Chuck Esau, "and fly back tomorrow. I'll land here."

I knew Mitchel pretty well, and it was no big deal for me to find the active runway by making a couple of passes with my wing landing lights. Bitter anger rose in my throat as I contemplated the utter stupidity of Colonel Johnson's blackout. Was he trying to destroy my squadron? Take revenge for my being at Mitchel? Why would he risk the lives of my crews? By the time my tires brushed the concrete I was sizzling to get hold of him, preferably by the throat.

I taxied up in front of Operations, cut the engines, and ran into the office with murder in my heart. "Where's Colonel Johnson?" I demanded.

"He's not in his office," said the duty officer. "Perhaps he's in his quarters."

Probably in the stable saddling his horse, I thought as I hurried out. It was a good run to the C.O.'s quarters, and the exercise cooled my head a bit. He was home, all right. "Colonel, you endangered my whole flight by cutting out the runway lights," I accused.

He cleared his throat importantly. "Well, Major, I'm not going to give a lighted target to the enemy. Pearl Harbor was lesson enough not to be surprised."

I said more, and used little tact. But it was no use. The old man was adamant, and obviously convinced he had done the right thing.

By morning some of my anger had drained off as I contemplated a court-martial. If the 20th was to continue operating with some degree of effectiveness at Mitchel I'd have to mend my fences. Calling at Colonel Johnson's office I saluted and ate crow: "Colonel, I apologize for my behavior last night. I was worried about the safety of my crews." He grunted and accepted my apology. Charges against me were never preferred. Needless to say, however, my relations with the base commander at Mitchel went from cool to frigid, and thereafter I managed to schedule patrols that returned well before dark.

A few days later I was also in trouble with the Navy. Each

morning we were given the colors of the day from the Eastern Sea Frontier. When we flew over a friendly naval vessel it was supposed to use a Very pistol to shoot up the right combination of colored flares. Our crews had had no training in the identification of naval craft, and without the colors they couldn't tell a French cruiser from an American destroyer.

One morning I received a call from an angry Navy officer. "One of your airplanes has bombed one of our destroyers!"

I gulped and visualized an American destroyer going down, a victim of our 100-pound bombs. When he told me it was a miss I thanked God that our bombardiers hadn't been fully trained. I promised to check it out immediately and call him back. Soon the B-25 on patrol landed and I summoned the crew. They were highly excited. "It was definitely a French destroyer," the pilot insisted, "because no colors of the day were displayed." The 100-pound bombs had landed near enough to the bow of the vessel to shake it up and drive it into wild evasive maneuvers.

I called back to Eastern Sea Frontier. "Yes," I admitted, "one of our B-25s dropped bombs near a destroyer, but the pilot says that the ship did not display the colors of the day. Did the ship reporting the bombing display the colors?"

There was a long pause. "No," he admitted, "it didn't."

"Well," I said, "why then are you giving us identification colors each morning?" There was no reply.

I reported the incident to my Air Force headquarters, but heard not another word from the Navy. After that, however, the colored recognition flares quickly shot aloft from all U.S. Navy craft whenever we came near. The Army Air Force had finally got the Navy's attention.

Fears of sabotage were everywhere. One day we were provided with the astonishing intelligence that an agricultural field had been plowed near us with an arrow pointing at Mitchel Field. The fact that Mitchel was accurately located on thousands of free road maps was entirely irrelevant. We were not permitted to perform night maintenance on our aircraft until we painted the hangar windows black. Indeed, the large headquarters in New York was finding much to do, and Colonel Johnson's blackout orders persisted. Such idiotic policies only hampered our operations, since any enemy night bombing raid could have easily spotted the black hole that was Mitchel Field.

Although we never found the French fleet, another enemy did show up off Long Island. We saw the evidence in several ships resting on the shallow ocean bottom. The first was the *Cyclops,* sunk off Cape Cod with eighty-seven lives lost. The German U-boats had arrived. They sank thirteen more vessels along the East Coast in January.

We patrolled diligently up and down the coast but the U-boats eluded us, surfacing only at night. Our patrols were the ultimate in tedium. Usually there was nothing to see but endless expanses of boring ocean. Nevertheless one of our pilots, 1st Lt. Louis M. Abernathy, gained lasting fame by radioing, "Sighted sub, sank same." His message made all the headlines. The succinct report rivaled "praise the Lord and pass the ammunition," which some chaplain had used at Pearl Harbor. Losing everywhere, the American public was frantic for any tidbit of good news. Unfortunately the reported U-boat sinking was never confirmed by the Navy.

Administrative matters consumed most of my time at Mitchel. It was a running fight with Colonel Johnson to get even minimal services for the squadron. Crews worked and flew odd hours and often went without meals, sometimes being turned away from the mess halls because they were wearing flying clothes instead of "Class A" uniforms. The old Army was still running the Air Corps.

We needed barracks, messing facilities, officers' quarters, offices, transportation for our crews, supply rooms, and hangar space to work on our B-25s. We were not organized to do our own maintenance, post our own guards, and handle the thousand and one tasks that the base was charged with doing. But we had to make do, because support from the base was indeed niggardly.

Enemy submarines sank more and more shipping and our mission intensified. Unfortunately the B-25 wasn't much of a sub hunter. Its two big engines drank so much fuel that we had little range—and no radars, of course. Nor did we have depth charges. The 100-pound bombs we carried had a perverse tendency to ricochet off the water and explode in the air beneath our bombers, so we didn't dare fly low, which would have been a good way to surprise surfaced U-boats.

We got no help from the Navy. Although they gave us operational orders, not a single blue-suiter visited our squadron. I suppose they knew little more than we did about how to hunt submarines from the air. It seemed that no preparations whatever had been made for such an air defense on the East Coast. We had to learn everything by trial and error.

We knew the U-boats were surfacing at night to do their dirty work, and after Colonel Johnson finally condescended to turn on the runway lights we tried night patrols, but with no success. We had no searchlights or flares that would illuminate a sub—and our limited range kept us from patrolling far enough out at sea to catch them on the surface in transit. Perhaps our most useful contribution was to keep the U-boats submerged in the daytime, making it somewhat more difficult for them to find and attack the coastal vessels. But it certainly wasn't enough. We were losing the battle.

The B-25s were not without the usual bugs found in new airplanes. One defect which plagued us was a high-pressure hydraulic hose that frequently burst and left us without power for flaps or landing gear. We had a couple of near accidents and were in dire need of stronger hoses. I sent wires like snowflakes to the matériel depot at Middletown, Pennsylvania, informing them of the unsatisfactory hoses. But only the same defective hoses were provided as replacements.

Finally I lost patience with the supply system. My alert

supply officer told me the Air Corps hadn't even ordered any stronger hoses yet.

"Where are they made?" I asked him.

"Air Associates, a factory in New Jersey."

"Well, that's not too far away. Get in your jeep, find that factory, and buy us the kind of hoses we need. Sign anything on my authority."

He returned the next day, his jeep loaded with stronger hoses, and we began to refit the hydraulic systems on our B-25s.

Going out of channels like this was a grievous military sin. Inspectors descended upon me from matériel headquarters. But I had kept a complete file of the many "unsatisfactory reports" we had submitted, and this file saved me from any disciplinary action.

Before all the airplanes had been refitted I became a victim of one of the burst hoses myself. Paradoxically it turned out to be a stroke of luck. I was patrolling off Cape Hatteras and scheduled to refuel at Langley Field before returning to Mitchel. It was the day before Christmas, and I was looking forward to seeing my wife and two kids for a brief visit.

As I made the approach and extended the gear we lost hydraulic pressure. The gear refused to latch in place. The wheels would move neither up nor down, even with the manual crank. We jettisoned our bombs "safe," so they wouldn't explode, in the Chesapeake Bay and I climbed to 6,000 feet, stalled and shook the airplane, tried tight turns. No joy. We faced a landing in which the gear would collapse and we'd slide down the runway on the ship's belly. Fire could possibly follow. It wasn't a happy prospect.

The B-25 gear retracted rearward and extended in a forward arc against the slipstream. Air pressure against the gear kept it from latching in the down position with its own weight. But I reasoned that if I could land sufficiently tail low, the forward force that would be exerted on the gear when it hit might snap it into the locked position. It was worth a try. Our fuel gauge read zero, and we had to get on the ground.

We came in just above a stall and dragged the tail before the gear touched. As the nose sank the gear snapped forward and the green lights came on. We taxied in with the fire trucks and ambulance and cut the engines.

Elise, all smiles and beautiful, was there on the flying line to meet me. Beside her was small son Kort, jumping up and down, and laughing baby Voan. My embrace of Elise was enhanced by Kort's and Voan's leg hugs. It was good to be home, and it would take at least a day to repair my B-25. Merry Christmas! Later I had considerable trouble convincing my friends that this stop at Langley had been caused by an emergency.

In our quarters Elise had tastefully decorated a tree beneath which were dozens of presents. My presents to them were still in the mail from Mitchel, but it didn't matter. Our Christmas celebration had a poignant warmth, with the ominous future hanging over us like a dark cloud.

Back at Mitchel I was awakened a little after dawn on New Year's Day by a thunderous explosion. I called Ops. "One of your B-25s went in off the end of the runway and blew up." My heart sank as I hastily dressed and ran to the flying line.

Lt. Charles Van Eeuwen had taken off at dawn with a full load of fuel, 100-pound bombs, and a crew of four besides himself. Eyewitnesses reported that after he had gained a hundred feet or so one of his two engines cut out, and apparently he couldn't maintain his altitude. So he deliberately dived his B-25 into a deep quarry where the bombs exploded. When I arrived there wasn't much left to identify in the smoldering wreckage.

Obviously Van had sacrificed himself and his crew to avoid crashing into the heavily built-up residential area of New Hyde Park near Mitchel Field. The people in the community were grateful and held a memorial service for him and his four brave crewmen, but that was little consolation to me. Freckle-faced Van had frequently been my copilot. About a year earlier, on a particularly hairy flight from Spokane to Salt Lake City, our four-engined B-17 Flying Fortress, which was going to be delivered to the British, had iced up over the Rocky Mountains. Luckily deicer boots and carburetor heat kept us afloat. So Van was an experienced pilot. I wondered why he hadn't dropped his bombs "safe" on that fateful New Year's Day of 1942. That would have lightened his load enough for the B-25 to climb on one engine. But Van had had little experience with live bombs—none, in fact, until we started carrying them at Mitchel. And perhaps he didn't even want to drop "safe" bombs on the residential community.

After the crash I was ordered to report to Maj. Gen. John K. Cannon, who was First Air Force commander now and in charge of all the Army Air Corps outfits on the East Coast. Order was being restored after the chaos of December 8.

I had never met "Uncle Joe" Cannon and didn't quite know what to expect, but instead of dressing me down for not adequately training the crew, or for poor maintenance that had caused the engine to fail, or for any number of other failings he could easily have found, he talked to me like a compassionate father who knew how much I was suffering the loss of five good airmen. "You must expect many such losses in the days ahead," he advised, "and you should try not to become too emotionally involved. Otherwise you will not be able to do your job." It was good, if hard, advice.

It soon became clear that B-25s simply weren't the war-planes for dealing with submarines, and I suppose the French fleet was finally located still safely berthed in Toulon. Late in January we were ordered back to Langley Field.

From Mitchel we flew back in style, a tight formation, even penetrating a heavy weather front en route. The silver birds were tucked in around me like flies to sugar. Each B-25 held its position through the clouds and we emerged into brilliant sunshine just short of Langley. My heart swelled with pride for these fine men, who had worked so devotedly at keeping the 20th in the air on its futile search for U-boats. How I wished I could take them into combat. Although our guns had never been fired in anger and we had rarely dropped a bomb, we felt we had been at war and were ready for larger responsibilities.

It was good to be home, under the able command of Col. Darr H. Alkire, who headed the 2nd Bomb Group. And it was almost a forgotten pleasure to serve on a base with a friendly base commander who knocked himself out to help us.

3
Hunting U-Boats

Admiral Karl Doenitz's U-boats had found a happy hunting ground along the East Coast, sinking hundreds of thousands of tons of merchant shipping while rarely losing a submarine to our puny antisubmarine efforts. By the end of January thirty-one ships of nearly 200,000 tons had been torpedoed. In February the U-boats sank sixty-nine ships in American waters, totaling over 350,000 tons. And the toll continued to grow. America's "arsenal of democracy," the vast wartime industrial effort that was then gearing up, was losing its momentum and threatening to come to a standstill.

In *The Hinge of Fate*, Winston Churchill wrote: "The protection afforded by the United States Navy was for several months inadequate. It is surprising indeed that during two years of the advance of total war toward the American continent more provisions had not been made against this deadly onslaught." That is precisely what we in the 20th were thinking as we struggled unsuccessfully with inappropriate weapons and tactics to halt these Nazi depredations.

Churchill became very agitated and sent repeated messages to FDR, calling this Battle of the Atlantic the most crucial of the war. Leaders in Washington were frantic, and grasped at every scheme imaginable, no matter how cockeyed, to check the Nazi onslaught. But only a few of their ideas worked.

Convoys of merchantmen with surface escorts and air cover had proved most successful for the British—perhaps the least unsuccessful would be a better way to put it—but it took months for the United States to organize such a system. And even more time was needed to get coastal communities to black out—or at least dim out—so that their lights wouldn't silhouette the freighters for the U-boat skippers. The fighting overseas filled our newspapers, and the public scarcely realized how serious the war close to home had become.

Having been the first squadron to confront the Nazi boats, no matter how ineffective we had been, the 20th became the center for testing many of the experimental weapons and devices then being developed by the scientific community. Our patrolling suffered as the 20th was charged with testing more and more of the experimental devices and ideas. None of them helped us at that stage of the war.

Some few of the gadgets, such as the sonobuoy, eventually became useful. When dropped from an airplane, the sonobuoy floated and listened for submarine propeller sounds, which were transmitted by radio to the circling airplane. But this device didn't tell where the sub was, and without a surface vessel to track down the enemy boat with other sound gear, we in the air didn't learn much more than we had already known. A sub was in the vicinity—but where?

Another device that had some potential for locating a submerged submarine was based upon the induction coil principle: if a coil of wires is passed over a metal object, a current of electricity will be induced in the coil. The electrical charge is proportional to the number of loops in the coil, and to get a charge sufficiently great to register when passing over a submerged submarine, thousands of loops were required.

A West Point classmate, Ralph Bucknam, who had resigned on graduation to become a patent lawyer, was commissioned a major and sent to Langley with a prominent scientist, one Dr. Howard Aiken, to work on this project. We gave them an old

YB-17 and they began to string fine wire around the wings in hundreds of coils. When they had finished, the bulging coils of wire on the leading and trailing edges of the wings were flared with aluminum skin and it became time to test the contraption.

The configuration of the wings had been drastically altered, and I had my doubts that the airplane would get off the ground, but when I charged down the runway the big bird lifted into the air as if nothing had been changed. So we learned that the multiwired YB-17 would fly; but could it locate a submerged U-boat?

We flew the big bomber over a derelict auto and the needle flickered nicely. Success! However, its effective range was determined to be something on the order of 300 feet. If we flew as low as 100 feet this gave us about 200 feet of range under water, which was too little to be practical. A U-boat could dive deeper than that. We never found a sub with it.

Nevertheless the idea was the forerunner and directly responsible for the follow-up effort by the National Defense Research Council, which resulted in a more sensitive device, using vacuum tubes to enhance the signal. When used in connection with surface craft, this had some later success. It was called MAD, for Magnetic Airborne Detector.

While I was still at Mitchel I had been asked to test out a drug which might be useful for crews. The drug was supposed to sharpen alertness and lessen fatigue. We were flying so many patrols that there was no doubt about our being fatigued, but I didn't like using my crews as guinea pigs. So I agreed to try the drug on myself but refused to issue it to the crews. I suppose it was some kind of amphetamine, but little was known about such drugs then.

On my next patrol I took two of the little white pills, at the same time briefing my copilot to keep an eye on me in the event I acted oddly or flew erratically. A half hour later I was on cloud nine. My mind was sharp; my coordination perfect. I actually enjoyed the patrol. The whitecaps below were beautiful. Nor did I have a hangover after landing. I reported all this to the medico who was running the experiment. Although that was the end of my participation in the experiment, years later I noticed that my flight surgeon was issuing "wake-up" pills to those few crews who needed a jump start in the morning.

What we really needed in the antisubmarine business was a good airborne radar that would permit us to locate the U-boats at a distance and surprise them before they could crash-dive. And we needed powerful flares and searchlights in order to spot the subs at night when they were surfaced and making their torpedo attacks. We also needed snub-nosed depth charges, instead of the 100-pound bombs that ricocheted. Most of all, we needed long-range, four-engined bombers that could fly far out to sea and catch the U-boats as they cruised on the surface across the Atlantic.

B-17Es were beginning to come off the production line, however, and periodically we received green crews to check out in an old YB-17 I had resurrected from the scrap heap. When an "E" arrived with its new high vertical fin and its lethal .50-caliber guns, and smelling of fresh paint, we'd give the new crews a few rides in the camouflaged "E" and then send them out across the South Atlantic en route to the Far East. It had taken me a year to check out in a B-17; now we had to do the job in days, with kids right out of flying school. It was a deadly game of catch-up, and at least one of the inexperienced crews never arrived in Africa.

In the meantime the U-boats continued to have a field day. Merchantmen were being torpedoed at night almost within sight of Langley Field. It was very embarrassing. I put an old B-18 bomber on alert, loaded with landing flares and 100-pound bombs. One night we got word that a ship had just been attacked off Cape Charles, less than a half hour from Langley. I fired up the old bomber and flew out to the coordinates where the attack had occurred. Then we began dropping flares. I found that nothing on the surface of the sea could be seen with those flares except in the line of reflection between the flare and the airplane, like the reflection on water between you and the moon. Desperately I attempted to circle the flares in order to see a wide sweep of the sea, and on one pass my heart jumped as a surfaced submarine momentarily appeared in the reflection. We dropped more flares and I circled wildly, attempting to locate the U-boat again and get set up for a bomb run. But the flares didn't last long enough and I was never able to find the boat. No doubt it had crash-dived when the flares and engine noise had advertised our presence. How I wished we had longer-burning flares and a powerful searchlight. Radar, too, would have been a big help.

Another of my West Point classmates, a close friend, was stationed at Langley. Ed Flanick and I had been assigned to the same outfits ever since graduation from the Academy. He was the group armament officer now, and had built an elaborate and effective gunnery range with moving targets. His brilliant mind found ways to overcome many of our problems with guns, bombsights, and munitions, and he had arranged to get us snub-nosed depth charges. I had flown with him often and knew him to be a superb and precise pilot, never in doubt as to the right maneuver. He often showed up at the 20th volunteering to fly a patrol.

On the fifth of March I lent him my old YB-17 and crew to patrol off Cape Hatteras, where the U-boats were most active. We hadn't yet received the snub-nosed depth charges, and my plane was loaded with the old 100-pound bombs. For a few hours we received position reports from Ed, and then silence. When he became overdue we sent out search planes. I flew one of these sweeps in a B-25. There wasn't a trace of wreckage where Ed had been last heard from, or where he might have gone down on his planned track. We searched for four days downwind of his track and then gave it up.

As someone remarked about B-17s at the start of the war, "Queens die proudly." Had Ed had engine trouble or even an engine fire, he would have had time to send an SOS or a verbal Mayday. But he simply vanished. I suspect that he was blown up by his own bombs when he attacked a U-boat as it was diving. Had a sub shot him down, he might still have had time to send a distress signal.

By April our B-25s were all gone, and we were flying a variety of old birds, but principally the B-18A, a lumbering twin-engined bomber. Now and then we managed to keep a B-17E for a time and schedule it on patrols. Convoys with protecting Navy surface craft were now being run, and we often covered them. Orbiting over the convoy hour after hour was boring duty, but it kept the U-boats submerged. We became experts with the Aldes blinker lamp, and carried on conversations with our surface charges to give us something to do.

It was exciting when we ran across sailors in rafts from sunken merchant ships. Oh, were they happy to see us! We'd toss them cans of water and rations tied to inflated life vests and radio their position to the Navy, then orbit over them until help arrived or we ran low on fuel.

The well-known author Paul Gallico visited Langley in July to help recruit bombardiers. He rode on a few patrols with us. To the delight of our crews, his short story "Bombardier," describing one of these rescue missions, was published in the August 15, 1942, issue of the *Saturday Evening Post*.

By the end of May I had been kicked upstairs and made executive officer of the group, second in command to Col. Darr Alkire. Much to my surprise I had received the silver leaves of a lieutenant colonel in December, and now, with the rapid expansion of the Army Air Forces, I found myself to be rather senior. By then, however, the 20th had been so knocked around that it hardly resembled the tightly run, well-trained outfit of December 7. So I didn't shed many tears on losing my command.

About this time we were assigned a Consolidated LB-30.

This was the lend-lease version of the fat four-engined Liberator bomber that later became the B-24. It had more range than the B-17, and was less in demand by the expanding Eighth Air Force in England. With some modifications it could become an excellent sub fighter.

First, however, we needed a good radar. Physicists at MIT in Boston had developed a 10-centimeter radar that would fit in the position of the ball turret and provide excellent definition of surface objects. In June I flew our LB-30 to Boston, where a "breadboard model" of this new radar was installed in our bomber. What a wonderful aid this radar was! Now we could locate a U-boat miles away, day or night, and fly directly toward it. But it was months before this radar could be manufactured and installed in new B-24s.

In a few encounters the U-boat didn't crash-dive but remained on the surface and elected to shoot it out with the attacking bomber. The German skippers soon learned that we had minimum forward firepower—an almost useless flexible .30-caliber gun—while a turret with twin .50s rested silently in the tail. I flew our LB-30 to the depot at Middletown, Pennsylvania, where my good friend Al Boyd was now in command, and suggested that the turret with the heavy guns be moved from the tail to the nose. He had it done in record time. Now we had a real sub hunter, and eventually B-24s so configured, designated as B-24Ds, would be coming our way.

I flew my first nine-hour patrol in a B-24D on June 1, 1943. Either then or shortly thereafter I had my first eyeball-to-eyeball encounter with a submarine.

We were about four hundred miles off Cape Hatteras when the radar operator reported: "I've got a contact. Twelve miles, fifteen degrees right. Could be another fishing boat—or a U-boat."

"Roger," I replied, easing the big four-engined ship into a shallow turn. One didn't make sharp banks when flying at 50 feet above an angry storm-tossed sea and through scud that forced us in and out of low wispy clouds.

I pushed the throttles forward and called for the bomb bay doors to be opened. "Let's hope this is for real," I announced over the interphone. "Bomb on the first pass if it is." I didn't expect to see a sub; we had been disappointed so many times.

As we emerged from a low cloud, the bombardier yelled, "I see it! It's a sub! It's a sub!"

My heart leaped. Was it possible that we'd finally get a crack at one of Hitler's vicious wolves? Then I too saw it in the misty distance. I prayed we could close the gap before he dove.

Our orders were to attack any submarine in our patrol area. But I had been studying silhouettes of submarines and this one didn't exactly look like a U-boat. Intelligence had cautioned that some U-boats had been known to disguise their superstructure to look like American boats, however, and I wasn't going to be taken in by that ploy.

We roared in to attack, heading up the submarine's wake, approaching its stern. From this angle it was hard to get a good look at its superstructure. Between the ocean spray and scuddy clouds we couldn't see much, anyway.

I searched the sky for recognition flares. The colors of the day were yellow and red, and all American Navy vessels should have had that code. If it were a friendly, it should be firing yellow and red flares like crazy. But there were none.

Yet I could see that it wasn't diving. This was unusual behavior. Then I recalled from briefings by Navy experts that in very rough seas such as it was encountering today, subs sometimes turned turtle when crash-diving, and preferred to take their chances on the surface. I was pretty sure the Nazis, who hadn't yet encountered the B-24D, believed we had little forward firepower and that we carried only depth charges, which might do less damage if the boat remained surfaced.

As we raced at full throttle toward the bomb release point,

the sub grew larger. I was moments away. Was it a U-boat or one of ours? I had to decide. If I let him go he'd probably sink a half-dozen ships and kill hundreds of American seamen.

Why wasn't he firing at me? I squeezed the button on my interphone mike and cried, "Don't bomb! Don't bomb!" I simply couldn't take the chance of sinking one of our own.

We flew over the conning tower and looked down at white faces. I circled to the left to make another run on the plunging sub, all the while studying the sky for recognition flares. He *did* look like a friendly, but was I being deceived? Where were the flares?

Again we lined up for the bomb run along his wake. "This time, if we see no flares," I said, "let him have it."

Just before we reached the bomb release point, up popped red and yellow flares. All the breath and tension drained from us as we realized how close we had come to sinking one of our own. We circled a few times, exchanged arm waves with the men in the conning tower, and continued on our patrol.

Two weeks later I was working in my office when a Navy commander called. He shook my hand warmly and with a look of glowing gratitude said, "Colonel, I had to look you up to thank you for saving my life and the lives of my crew. You had every right to sink us. My boat had nothing but trouble in a patrol off the African coast. Communications were bad and we were way off on our navigation. We were in the wrong place at the wrong time.

"You caught us by surprise and when I tried to fire the rec-ognition flares nothing happened. They'd got wet and wouldn't ignite. I had to send below to find dry ones. It was touch and go before you came around on your second pass."

In hundreds of hours of ocean patrolling from the air, that was as close as I ever came to sinking a submarine.

Up to July of 1942, only six U-boats had been sunk in North American waters. That month found us doing a little better as five were destroyed off the Atlantic coast, half by convoy escorts, air and surface. New enemy boats coming into service each month exceeded the rate of our kills, however, and over 400,000 gross tons were sent to the bottom by the Nazis in each of our worst months of May and June 1942. After that shipping losses began to taper off somewhat as fully organized, well-protected convoys came into general use. During July less than 100,000 tons of shipping were lost in American waters. The threat was still formidable, but it seemed that we were slowly learning how to deal with the elusive enemy.

The U.S. Navy was so heavily committed in the Pacific that it appeared the Army Air Forces would have to provide the land-based antisubmarine effort in the Atlantic for an indefinite period. It was clear that we weren't properly organized for this kind of warfare. It took too long to get operational orders through the many headquarters so that a patrol could be launched. Intelligence was so slow that when it arrived it was almost ancient history. What we needed was a specialized major headquarters, adjacent to the Navy's Eastern Sea Frontier at 90 Church Street in New York City. We were eager to cooperate with the Navy, but there was no organization that would make this close association possible.

The Navy was keeping good track of Admiral Doenitz's boats as they cruised across the Atlantic from the Bay of Biscay off the west coast of France. The German admiral insisted that his boats check in every night by radio, and with this excellent information we were beginning to call our shots and at least keep most of the boats submerged. We needed a headquarters that could directly order any squadron on the East Coast to investigate a contact or a sinking, and also to arrange for leapfrog coverage of convoys.

I was called to New York on several occasions to work with others in designing just such a unique organization for hunting

U-boats and protecting our shipping. Colonel Fowler, a bomb group commander in New England, and I (I now commanded the 2nd Bomb Group) recommended that the group organizations be eliminated, thus doing ourselves out of our prestigious jobs and possible promotions. The idea was accepted, and the Army Air Forces Antisubmarine Command began its gestation. I was then ordered to New York City, with duty station at the Federal Building, 90 Church Street. We occupied two whole floors of that great building.

The Henry Hudson Hotel provided reasonable rates for all the Air Force personnel assigned to the new AAF Antisub headquarters and I lived there on temporary duty for some weeks while we went to work ironing out all the wrinkles of our new command. I was appointed assistant chief of staff, A-4 (supply and matériel), to Maj. Gen. Westside T. "Swede" Larson, the commanding general, and given an impressive office in the corner of the thirteenth floor, with great windows that looked out over lower Manhattan and the Hudson River. Below my window the huge new French luxury liner *Normandie* lay on its side. Saboteurs had set it on fire and it sank right there by the dock, where it remained as a constant reminder that the war was close to home.

I didn't want Elise to move to crowded New York with the kids. I expected soon to get an overseas assignment and it would be better in the meantime for her and the kids to remain at Langley. When my orders overseas came I hoped she would move to Reno near my parents, where my brother Thor's wife and family had decided to live while he served in England. But this idea didn't appeal to her.

As the weeks and then months dragged by without my receiving orders, Elise began to take this separation as a rejection and I agreed to her moving to New York. Just before Christmas, 1942, she and the two kids joined me and we found an apartment on Long Island's Jackson Heights.

It wasn't a happy arrangement. I worked long hours. The U-boats had no regard for regular hours or weekends. Frequent TDYs took me away from home. Kort and Voan, who had been used to all outdoors at Langley, were now confined to a cramped apartment with limited play space. And Kort was developing a squint in one eye which worried us.

That winter the Red Cross informed Elise that her beloved older brother, an infantry officer who had been stationed in the Philippines, had died in the Bataan death march. It was a devastating blow to her, and she railed at the unfairness and cruelty of war.

Each day I commuted to work on the subway, even while it seemed that all my contemporaries were serving in active theaters of war. I was committed to fighting for my country wherever told to do so, but this seemed a strange way to do it.

4
Getting Overseas

y early 1943 the AAF Antisubmarine Command had arranged for a string of air bases it could use stretching from Newfoundland to Cuba. We were soon given a directive to hunt submarines anywhere in the Atlantic, and we were planning to send squadrons to North Africa and England. Thus our bombers would never be far from a convoy or a marauding U-boat.

It was my job to inspect these bases, to assure that they were providing the necessary services to our squadrons. We intended to permit no more glitches like the one I had experienced at Mitchel, and we managed to obtained a lengthy circular from the commanding general of the Army Air Forces detailing just what services the bases were obliged to perform.

Our headquarters was assigned a few low-powered, twin-engined utility craft called the UC-78, which were based at Mitchel, and I made my inspections in those ugly and ungainly birds, including a February trip to Cuba. It was a welcome respite from frigid New York.

Our diplomats had arranged for us to build a modern airport near Havana, which we named Batista Field in honor of the then-dictator, Fulgencio Batista, and we had landing rights. I enjoyed the Latin ambience of Havana, and of course it was necessary to visit Sloppy Joe's famous bar. I also flew to Boca Chica and de los Banos at the eastern end of the island, where we had communication stations attempting to pick up signals from surfaced U-boats and locate their positions. The boats were now moving southward toward the Caribbean, where we had poor coverage.

Shortly after this trip one of our patrolling B-18s made a fuel stop at Batista and headed back to Miami after dark. Something went terribly wrong and the bomber never made landfall, nor did anyone receive an SOS or a Mayday. When we learned that the B-18 was overdue we immediately instituted the usual search, but no sign was ever found of the bomber or crew.

A few days later a young second lieutenant, a signal officer, showed up at our headquarters with a fabulous tale. He was an officer assigned to one of our listening stations in Cuba, and was on leave. He had been deadheading back to the States in the B-18 that had vanished.

Here, miraculously, was a lone survivor. I called him in to learn what had happened. He told me that he suspected that the pilot and copilot had visited Sloppy Joe's, because they didn't look too sharp. However, he was anxious to get home and decided to take a chance by flying with them.

"I'm no navigator," he said, "but after flying several hours and not seeing the lights of southern Florida, I knew we were headed out to sea. I was riding in the back of the plane and couldn't call the pilot because he was on the radio. I began to get real scared and strapped on a parachute. We kept right on flying into the black darkness ahead and there wasn't a light anywhere. I had no idea how long we could fly, but when I heard an engine sputter I figured we were running out of gas. So I decided my best bet was to bail out.

"I hit the water pretty hard but managed to get out of my chute harness and inflate my Mae West. It was pitch dark but the water wasn't cold. I had no idea where I was. I figured if the sharks didn't get me I could survive until daylight and then maybe see some land or something.

"After hanging in my Mae West for maybe an hour I saw the running lights of a big boat heading right toward me. I began yelling at the top of my lungs and kept it up. That's why I'm still a little bit hoarse. It was a tanker and the lookout spotted me. They picked me up and here I am."

I shook my head in amazement. "Did you see what happened to the B-18?" I asked.

"When I landed in the water it was nowhere in sight."

"Well, Lieutenant, I appreciate your coming in to give us this report," I told him. "The odds against your being rescued at night under such conditions were astronomical. You don't need to worry about surviving this war. With your kind of luck you'll live forever."

I spent a few days in May 1943 checking out in the new B-24D at Langley, and arranged to have six of them transferred to Jack Roberts's squadron located at Port Lyautey just north of Casablanca in North Africa. Jack was having considerable success hunting the U-boats between the Canary Islands and the Strait of Gibraltar, and we wanted him to have the latest equipment. It had been almost a year since I had visited Al Boyd with the LB-30 and recommended specifications for a worthy sub hunter. Now the B-24Ds were coming off the production lines in profusion.

I managed to talk General Larson into letting me lead the flight of six B-24Ds to North Africa, and I decided to load four 325-pound depth charges in my bomber in case we happened to sight a U-boat on the way. We took off on June 15 from Langley and landed at Homestead Field near Miami for the cross-Atlantic briefing, conducted by the Air Transport Command that ran the very active southern Atlantic route. I had prescience enough to collect a case of booze by visiting one liquor store after another—it was rationed, one bottle to a customer. I was sure that this would be a welcome gift for Jack Roberts and his people, whose living conditions were pretty primitive.

On June 17 we flew to Borinquen Field in Puerto Rico, and from there to Waller Field in Trinidad on the nineteenth. We had to leave one of our B-24s behind at Borinquen because of engine trouble, but it caught up with us before we reached our destination. From Trinidad we paralleled the South American coast, flying southeast over the Amazon jungle, and I looked down into the impenetrable green canopy that hid a few Air Force planes that hadn't made it. On this leg we penetrated the stationary equatorial front with its torrential rains, and I wondered how our big engines could still run in that deluge. But I was in high spirits and hummed the popular samba "Brazil" as we let down to land at Belém, on the vast mouth of the muddy Amazon River. That evening I went shopping for a large aquamarine stone that I planned to give to Elise.

The next day we made the six-and-a-half-hour flight to Natal, on the easternmost tip of Brazil. This was the jumping-off place for the south Atlantic crossing. Two things happened there. I had a flight with the Air Transport Command people, who wanted me to download my depth charges in order to lighten our plane. The twelve-hour crossing would require all the fuel we could carry, and my gross weight was over the limit, something like 80,000 pounds. I won that argument, but agreed that the other B-24s in my flight need not carry the bombs. However, I was determined to have the wherewithal to attack a U-boat if we should run into one. I had won an Air Medal for several hundred hours of antisubmarine patrolling, but had yet to get a good shot at a U-boat.

The other development was the increased value of the booze I had stashed in our airplane. I was offered fifty dollars a bottle by some locals who had learned about it. It seemed like a wise move to post our own guard on the bird, and my combat crew got the duty.

We took off at night into a rainstorm, and I was not a little concerned about the heavy B-24 lifting off the runway. But it took to the air like the proverbial homesick angel, and we charged into the face of the frightening equatorial front. Rain fell in sheets and made a thundering drumbeat on the skin of our bird. I could see nothing beyond our navigation lights. Hours later the rain slackened and the faint light of dawn revealed the broad expanse of grey ocean beneath us. I sighed in relief.

As we neared Africa I called Dakar for a weather report and got my first taste of British taciturnity. In America the response would have described the weather. But the British radio operator simply replied, "The weather is fit."

Dakar was a dusty frying pan. Accommodations were miserable, and I resolved to leave that crude station as soon as possible. Fortunately some guards, called "wogs" in the local vernacular, as black as silhouettes, were put on our B-24s and I had no fear of our booze being hijacked, although by then its value had climbed to a hundred dollars a bottle.

It took us eight hours to fly north over the Sahara Desert to Marrakech. An enormous sandstorm obscured the ground and tinged the air tan, but we were able to fly over most of it. Marrakech was a delight. We stayed in a resort hotel and lounged on hassocks while turbaned waiters brought us drinks. On the twenty-seventh we made the hour-and-a-half flight to Port Lyautey, where Jack Roberts and his troops met us with open arms. They were ecstatic at receiving the six new B-24Ds, and knew that they could increase their score of kills with these capable bombers.

As soon as I was alone with Jack in his office I presented him the invaluable case of Miami booze. He gasped with pleasure. They had been several months with nothing more alcoholic than weak peanut beer. Jack immediately went to the squadron safe, opened it, and removed stacks of classified documents. Then he carefully packed the precious bottles in the safe and locked it—all except one bottle of Old Grand-Dad bourbon, which he opened, pouring two fingers each in thick water glasses. We toasted the AAF Antisubmarine Command, and "good hunting!"

While I was there Jack gave me a long shopping list of his squadron's needs. With most of the supplies being sent to the east where the battle had raged, his squadron was an orphan. I drove to Casablanca to talk with officials of the First Area Air Service Command and the Third General Depot. I found many of the items on Jack's list sitting right there in Casablanca warehouses. Needless to say, administration and supply procedures were not the best. Items that I couldn't find in Casablanca were included in an urgent message radioed to my office in New York. I knew they would have the supplies on the next available air transport.

Algiers was in Allied hands. Africa had been swept clean of the enemy after the resounding victory of the Allied forces at Tunis, when a quarter of a million Axis troops had surrendered. That had happened on May 12, less than two months before I had landed at Port Lyautey. Army Air Forces under Gen. Pete Quesada were now bombing Italy and I wanted to go on one of those missions. So I bummed a ride in a C-43 to Algiers, where Quesada had his headquarters.

Swarming with Allied troops, Algiers was still celebrating the victory, and the bar at the Hotel Alletti where I found a billet was filled with revelers. There was nothing to drink but *vin au glass*, although that didn't dim the celebrations. I ran into a former West Point football coach who told me they were there to plan the next operation. There was no dearth of charming French mademoiselles turned out in beautiful gowns and I struck up a conversation with one, buying her a *vin au glass* at exorbitant cost. I invited her to dinner, thinking she could steer me to a reputable place. Mais non! she said—not unless I was prepared to spend the night with her. I was stunned. Here was a

prostitute with all the polish and manners of a New York debu-
tante. Then I looked around the bustling lounge and realized
that most, if not all, of the lovely young women were pros-
titutes. War and hardship were no doubt at the root of their
circumstances. She quoted a price that would have left me
penniless for the rest of my trip. Regretfully I declined her
tempting offer. She could not accept my invitation for dinner
because, she explained, she must find a customer who could
afford the whole deal.

I made some supply calls and generally cooled my heels in
Algiers for four days, waiting for the ride on a combat mission
that General Quesada had promised me. Eventually I realized
that it was a hopeless quest and returned to Casablanca and then
to Marrakech, where I caught a ride on a big four-engined C-54
transport bound for Prestwick, Scotland. It was a twelve-hour
flight out to sea and around neutral Spain and enemy-occupied
France, but we flew at night and suffered only boredom.

A C-43 flight took me to Hendon Field, London, and there
my brother Thor met me. He was a lieutenant colonel on the
staff that was planning Overlord, the cross-channel invasion.
Thor checked me into the Cumberland Hotel near Marble Arch
and I phoned classmate Bill Gross, who was now a B-17 wing
commander at Bassingbourn. He would soon pin on the first
general's stars to be won by our West Point class of 1934. Bill
drove down to London and we had a grand reunion. Before Bill
had left the States for England I had checked him out in a B-17.
Now he was commanding three groups of them, over a hundred
bombers on three stations. I felt that the war was passing me by.

Later I checked in at Widewing, the Eighth Air Force
headquarters, to make arrangements for a flight to St. Eval on
the southwesternmost tip of England, where we had another
antisub squadron commanded by Lt. Col. Steve McElroy.
While at Widewing I ran into Bob Williams, who was now commanding the 1st Air Division of B-17s bombing *Festung Europa*,

and he again promised me command of one of his nine groups "if you can get yourself sprung from the Antisubmarine Command." I had a conference with Air Marshal Sir John Slessor, who commanded the RAF Coastal Command, and he advised me that the U.S. Navy was ready to assume the AAF Antisubmarine Command mission and that the Antisub Command would soon be broken up. So my chances looked pretty good.

Eighth Air Force provided me with an airplane and I flew down to St. Eval on the twelfth of July, with an en route stop at Portneath to check in with the RAF Coastal Command outfit that our squadron reported to. The next morning about 3:00 A.M. I went on a Bay of Biscay patrol in a B-24D. Steve McElroy granted me the honor of piloting the bird, while he flew as copilot. Just north of the coast of Spain we ran across some RAF Coastal Command bombers that had a submerged submarine contact and were dropping smoke buoys to mark his position. This was as close as we came to a U-boat.

On the way home, however, we spotted a speck far to our right that by examination through the binoculars turned out to be a JU-88. He was obviously attempting an interception. I feared that if the German ever caught us our Liberator would come out second best.

It occurred to me that he was already far from shore and might be concerned about his fuel supply; the JU-88 was not a long-range airplane. Perhaps I could lure him further out to sea and cause him to burn up too much fuel in the wide-open chase. So we turned due west, opened the throttles wide, and put the B-24 in a shallow dive. I had never before known how fast that bird could fly. It scooted over the water like a diving falcon. The JU-88 continued to gain on us, but only slowly. Our gunners had charged their guns and fired warming bursts. The enemy craft never got close enough to fire his guns, and after what seemed like an hour or two but was probably no more than a few minutes he gave up, made a 180-degree turn, and headed back to Brest.

After that experience our navigator was somewhat confused, and when we made landfall I was doubtful that it was Land's End, England. I had heard about an Eagle squadron earlier in the war mistaking the Brest Peninsula for Land's End. All were shot down. So I broke radio silence and asked for a steer. Sure enough, the land we had sighted was the Brest Peninsula. If we had come much nearer, swarms of enemy fighters would have attacked us.

By the twentieth I was ready to go home, and Bill Gross flew me in a B-17F to Prestwick, Scotland, where I caught a C-54 to cross the North Atlantic. The flight was routine until I hooked a night flight from Presque Isle, Maine, to La Guardia, New York, in another C-54. It was loaded with engines that had not been tied down very securely. Over Boston we encountered a severe thunderstorm and the turbulent air thrashed our big bird around like a cat with a mouse. The heavy engines, which rested in the center of the fuselage just touching our knees, began to bounce up and down with terrifying crashes, while the airplane screeched and groaned as if it were coming apart. Here I was, almost home, and now this was the end. My luck had run out.

I was sure the bird could not take such punishment. A young second lieutenant sitting next to me on the bucket seats cupped his hands to my ear and said, "If I survive this war I'm going to build a cabin high in the Rocky Mountains and I hope to hell I never see another airplane for the rest of my life!" At that moment, them was my sentiments exactly.

Then like an answer to our prayers, the big bird flew out of the thunderstorm into smooth air.

5

First Mission

B ob Williams lived up to his word, and when the AAF
Antisubmarine Command broke up in the fall of
1943, I received orders transferring me from a desk in Manhattan to his 1st Air Division of the Eighth Air Force in England.
After a hasty and tearful good-bye to Elise and the children I
boarded a new DC-4 at La Guardia and crossed the North
Atlantic to Prestwick. Full of enthusiasm, I reported to Bob's
headquarters for two days of briefings on all aspects of the war. It
didn't look good, and my enthusiasm began to wane. Bob sent
me to Willie Hatcher's 351st Group for further orientation. After
a sleepless night during which I confronted the prospective
perils of the combat command I had always thought I wanted, I
prepared for my first mission.

My fears began to subside as I crawled into the nose of
Willie Hatcher's lead B-17 at Polebrook along with his cool lead
navigator and equally cool bombardier. These airmen demonstrated a calm professionalism as they busied themselves with
their equipment, charts, and graphs. A rush of admiration
swept through me for these brave men who had defied the
deadly Luftwaffe and flak gunners time and again. I began to
feel guilty that I had let my childish nighttime fears get the
better of me.

The air was crystal clear and bitterly cold as we crossed the North Sea on the way to Wilhelmshaven. During penetration of the German coast I flinched inwardly at each flak burst that dirtied the air around us with ugly "whumpfs." Trying my best not to reveal my anxiety, I charged the guns and fired warming bursts.

Soon our eighteen-plane groups took interval at the Initial Point for the bomb run, and here we became more vulnerable. Mutual supporting fire was diminished and we had to fly straight and level, taking no evasive action, in order to drop our bombs accurately. Of course the enemy knew this very well.

Flak peppered us unmercifully, bumping our craft with close explosions and rattling metal fragments against the fuselage. I imagined jagged steel slicing into my body. Then the flak stopped as enemy fighters charged in. I saw two Forts from other groups go down. One cripple from our group broke formation and surged erratically out in front of our lead ship. I could only imagine what had happened in the cockpit. Three crewmen dropped from the open bomb bay and their chutes blossomed. Then enemy fighters began following the big cripple to give it the coup de grace. Hanging on their props they pumped streams of hot fire into it.

My fear vanished. Seething with anger, I fired my .50 at the little jackals, but they were out of range. Suddenly the crippled Fort majestically rolled belly-up like a dead fish, dove, and burst into a ball of orange flame. As the fire cleared the debris fell in a cloud of smoke, with pieces so small it seemed that none was large enough to be a man. The great bomber simply disintegrated into dust as we passed over.

The harbor at Wilhelmshaven with its shipping and U-boat docks, our target, stood out clearly under the glare of the bright sun. "Bombs away," called the bombardier as the ship lurched up. The job was done and Clint Ball, the pilot, banked sharply, diving some to throw off the flak gunners. A sense of relief spread through me. We were on our way home. My relief was short-lived, however. The macabre fun was only beginning.

Great formations of enemy fighters appeared off our right wing. They queued up in single file, flying our way but out of range of our guns—ME-109s mostly, but a few FW-190s. The butterflies again fluttered in my stomach, as I stared in awe at this threatening foe.

The line of enemy fighters passed us, then when each was about a mile or two ahead he would reverse his course and fly directly at our nose, firing his guns all the way. Just when it seemed we would collide he would flip over on his back and dive in a half loop, then work his way back to the queue for another pass.

We had no friendly fighter escort that I could see, but with something like three hundred heavy .50-caliber guns tracking him it was no free ride for the enemy. This kind of frontal attack with a half roll was a popular Luftwaffe tactic in those days, but it proved costly to the Jerries. They faced a massive concentration of gunfire focused on each attack, as all the Forts in the assembled combat box of fifty-four aimed at each individual fighter making its head-on dash. I could actually see the cone of fire with the enemy at its apex, and I marveled at the courage of those German pilots, who could drive home their attacks against such a hail of death. The fire came not only from the flexible nose guns, one of which I was wildly shooting, but from the twin .50s in the upper turrets and other pairs of .50s in the ball turrets.

Strangely I was no longer frightened during these encounters. The bucking .50 in my hands was comforting. It kept me busy. I didn't fire short bursts, as we had been taught to do. Instead I held the trigger down with my thumbs and sprayed the fast-closing fighters with all I had.

One fighter I was tracking in began to smoke. No doubt dozens of guns were firing at it. He passed under us before I could tell whether he was mortally hit. Besides, I was busy firing at the next little bastard who came charging in spitting his lethal metal.

And so I was "blooded." Because I survived that first mission I learned that premonitions were simply a reflection of fear, and that perhaps I just might beat the odds and live through this war.

I flew another mission with Willie's group to Knaben, Norway, where we bombed a heavy-water plant to slow up Germany's atomic bomb development. There was little opposition—a piece of cake. So I decided against informing Bob Williams of my faintheartedness. Perhaps, after all, I could learn to control my emotions. Moreover, I never again allowed myself the luxury of idly lying awake at night. When I hit the sack thereafter, I made sure that I was almost too tired to stand. By working every waking moment, there would be no time to be frightened.

One's mind simply can't attend to more than one subject of concentration at the same time. So if I didn't think about the danger, the fear diminished. Moreover, familiarity with the danger, after I survived a number of missions, tended to give me the fatalism I needed—that sense of living a charmed life. If I took all necessary precautions, and drilled my group in flying a tight defensive formation while emphasizing gunnery training, then whatever happened was in the hands of the gods.

That first mission had taught me one major lesson, however, that would help to carry me through the next year of bloody warfare: to blanket fear, *keep busy.*

Before leaving New York, Elise and I had agreed to number our letters serially so that we could tell if any were missing. In the space of one month, as I moved from one headquarters to another, my APO (Army Post Office) number had changed three times and it must have confused Elise to keep up with the changes I sent her.

The APO was overburdened with mail and slow in forwarding letters. I received letters 1 and 2 while at Bob's headquarters and then the letters stopped coming. I wrote home almost every day and longed for word from Elise. After a couple of weeks I began to worry.

6

Hung Bomb

On November 23 Willie Hatcher lent me a dull khaki-painted Ford staff car and driver to take me to my new station. It was a dreary overcast day but I was hopped up with enthusiasm and anticipation. We drove through Kettering, a plain factory town, and on for the seven miles to the little thatched-roof village of Grafton Underwood. Then through the station gate, where a scruffy, lackadaisical corporal waved us through with no salute.

We continued through farmland on a muddy road for a few miles before arriving at the cluster of Quonset huts that housed the headquarters of the 384th Bomb Group (H)—the "H" stood for "heavy." There I was greeted by Col. Julius K. "Con" Lacey, the interim commander of the group, who was holding down the fort until I arrived. Bob Williams had Con slated to command a combat wing, and he was anxious to leave the 384th. I soon understood why. In the two months he had been there, the 384th must have ground him down, and his good reputation was threatened.

The change of command was the ultimate in simplicity. We shook hands, a picture was taken, we exchanged good wishes, and he climbed into a staff car and drove away. I walked into the cold office he had vacated—all English rooms seemed cold since they were "warmed" by tiny coke stoves that were hard to start and often went out—and began to get acquainted with my first assistant, the air exec, Lt. Col. William E. "Willie" Buck, Jr., a West Point graduate and the only other regular officer in the command. Also awaiting me there was the nonrated ground exec, Lt. Col. James A. Taff, who was responsible for everything but the flying part of our mission.

My first duty was to dictate an order: "GENERAL ORDER NUMBER 4 paragraph 1. Under the provisions of AR 600-20, the undersigned hereby assumes command of the 384th Bomb Group (H) and AAF Station No. 106. (signed) Dale O. Smith, Colonel. Air Corps, Commanding." Thus began the most challenging and terrifying year of my life.

Neither Buck nor Taff seemed particularly happy to see me, and I was puzzled. I doubted that they had any word of my reputation, good or bad. They were polite and proper, but that was all. Their coolness was palpable. I could see that it would take some doing to win their respect and confidence. Perhaps Willie Buck had expected to be given command of the group. He had been on board less than two months, having joined two weeks after Colonel Lacey had replaced the original group commander, Col. Budd J. Peaslee, on October 1. A short, well-built man with a serious manner, Willie Buck had a splendid combat record, as the ribbons on his chest testified.

No doubt Colonel Lacey had sought him out to help reorganize and revitalize the shot-up 384th. The job was far from accomplished, and I would have to lean heavily on Willie to help me complete the task.

The attitudes of the air and ground execs extended throughout the command. Everyone seemed to have a chip on his shoulder, and a sullen resentment of my intrusion. The 384th had experienced some of the most vicious fighting of the air war, and had suffered tragic and crippling losses. In the face of this they had conducted themselves with signal honor. But the nature of combat command is to achieve victory over the enemy, and this, in the eyes of the combat wing commander, Brig. Gen. Robert Travis, and the air division commander, Maj. Gen. Bob Williams, had not been achieved by the 384th. So their beloved group commander, Col. Budd Peaslee, who had led some of the roughest missions, had been relieved.

There wasn't a man who had served under Peaslee who didn't consider his relief an injustice. And here was this lanky Stateside colonel with practically no combat experience taking his place. I knew that I could never truly assume command until I had gained more combat experience, and I decided to fly the very next mission.

It was one of those impossibly cold winter days over Germany in 1943, November 26 to be exact, at 22,000 feet, when the thermometer registered as low as the instrument permitted and the rheostats on our electrically heated long johns, boots, and gloves were twisted to maximum. The gunners had to be particularly careful. If they removed their gloves to clear a jam, their hands would stick to the metal and frostbite was certain, with eventual loss of shriveled fingers.

Over the Bremen shipyards, just after bombardier Warren Parmer called "bombs away," radio operator Joe Purdy in the compartment aft of the Flying Fortress bomb bay reported with a note of controlled panic in his voice, "There's a hung bomb!" From that moment on our fortunes rapidly deteriorated.

Luckily I was flying with Siguard Thompson's excellent lead crew. I recalled again Bob Williams's staff talking about my need "to get blooded," and I knew more than ever what they meant now. This mission to Bremen with Sig Thompson was my first in a command position, although we were flying number two to Maj. Raymond P. Ketelsen, who led the group. Afterwards Sig said, "I can't remember ever sweating more when the temperature was about sixty below, and I kept thinking—this colonel picked a good one for his first and last mission."

"Bombardier from pilot," Sig called over the interphone. "Go back there and see if you can knock that hung bomb loose. The shackle's probably frozen." Any moisture at that temperature stopped a mechanism from working.

"Roger," replied Parmer as he laboriously untangled himself from the nose compartment, just in front of and below me. Disconnecting his oxygen and plugging the rebreather mask into a portable bottle, pulling the jacks on his electrical heat and interphone (we wouldn't hear from him until he plugged in again at another station), he had to squeeze up through the trapdoor behind the pilot and work his way around the top turret in his cumbersome, thick flying clothes. The process seemed to take forever. When he opened the hatch to the bomb bay, a roaring icy tempest filled the pilot's cabin. Precariously negotiating the nine-inch-wide catwalk through the bomb bay and steadying himself with its supports, he inched his way toward the dangling bomb. The yawning clamshell bomb bay doors revealed nothing below but grey clouds.

I lost sight of Parmer as he entered that violently screeching bomb bay. I prayed he wouldn't fall. Everyone knew how quickly those subzero winds could freeze a man, and he was wearing no chute. It would have been too awkward a job for anyone wearing a belly chute. After working on the stuck bomb shackle Parmer traversed the catwalk aft and plugged his interphone into a receptacle in the radio operator's compartment.

"Can't knock it loose, Sig," he called. "It's still hanging there."

My pulse began to beat a little faster. If that incendiary bomb exploded we'd be engulfed in a ball of fire. However, if it were still unarmed there was little danger.

The arming device on the nose of the bomb consisted of a sensitive fulminate of mercury fuse that caused the less volatile explosive in the bomb to detonate. The fuse was activated when a small vane on the nose of the bomb spun off as the bomb fell, so that the bomb would not be armed or hot until it was a safe distance below the airplane. When it was stowed on the shackles in the bomb bay, a safety wire kept the small vane from spinning off. The other end of the safety wire was secured to the bomb bay, and the wire would pull out of the fuse as the bomb fell, permitting the small vane to spin. If the wire was still secured to the nose of the bomb it was "safe." But if the wire had pulled out, the vane would spin off inside the bomb bay and arm the bomb. The slightest impact of the fuse on any part of the airplane would then cause the bomb to explode.

"How does it look?" I asked Parmer.

"One shackle released. It's hanging nose down. The rear shackle is stuck closed. I hammered it but it's jammed solid."

"How about the arming wire?"

"It's still in the fuse but pulling out. I'm going back and try to cut it." If he could cut the wire between the fuse and the bomb bay anchor the bomb would remain "safe."

"Be careful." What a senseless remark, I thought. Of course he'd be careful. I wished I could think of something reassuring to say.

Parmer was resourceful. He borrowed parachute harnesses from the two waist gunners, hooked them together and attached one end to his own harness and the other end to Joe Purdy's. Thus they were held together with a makeshift safety line like mountain climbers. Then he returned to the roaring subzero bomb bay.

Armed with a pair of heavy pliers and holding on to the catwalk supports he leaned far out to cut the arming wire. No joy. It was a tantalizing two inches out of reach. If he stretched out any farther he could lose his balance and drop through the open bomb bay, possibly pulling Joe Purdy after him. He banged the frozen shackle with the pliers a few more times. No luck. Purdy saw Parmer falter and dragged him back into the protected radio compartment before he lost consciousness. Then Purdy called, his voice losing some of its calm.

"The arming wire just pulled out of the fuse. The vane's turning."

My heart dropped to my boots. So this was it. Before I got my feet wet in my new job, we were going to be blown to kingdom come with our own bomb. It was slowly becoming armed. What to do now?

The meaning of Purdy's report was not lost on the crew. "Shall we bail out, Colonel?" someone called.

"Sit tight!" I ordered. "We're over the North Sea now. You wouldn't last ten minutes in that water."*

If I sent Parmer or Purdy back into the bomb bay I feared they would lose their balance in the numbing cold, or even cause the bomb to swing against a support and explode.

"The vane just spun off, Colonel," Purdy reported ominously from the door of the radio compartment. "The bomb is armed."

"Is it swinging much?" I asked. Fortunately the air was smooth, but with those cumulus clouds ahead that could change.

"A little," he said.

"Bombardier from copilot," I called. "Stay where you are. Don't go into the bomb bay again. Shut the hatch." The less air turbulence in the bomb bay the better. I didn't dare shut the bomb bay clamshell doors because they might strike the nose of the armed bomb.

Slowly, with infinite care and caution, Sig Thompson pulled away from the formation, which was now reduced from eighteen to thirteen birds with our triangle "P" tails. There was no sense in endangering other ships if we were about to blow up. Now we found ourselves alone in the still hostile sky. There was

---

* But others did. Maj. William F. Gilmore's Fort was so badly shot up he had to ditch in the Channel. Ten minutes later an RAF rescue boat found six of the crew in a rubber raft and pulled a seventh out of the water. The engineer, Tech. Sgt. Maurice V. Henry, who had helped everyone out of the sinking airplane, was never found. He was awarded the Distinguished Service Cross posthumously.

only one thing to do. Fly that big bird as smoothly as possible, avoiding clouds with turbulence, and let down into warmer air. With luck the shackle might thaw and the armed bomb would drop into the North Sea.

I took the controls of *Damn Yankee*. Perhaps I was no better a pilot than Sig Thompson, but I had a thousand more hours than he in B-17s and besides, I needed something to do.

"Crew from copilot," I called. "I'm going to fly as smoothly as I can and let down. Hold on. The bomb should drop in warmer air. Check in."

"Navigator, roger."

"Bombardier, roger."

"Engineer, roger."

"Right waist gunner, roger."

"Left waist, roger."

"Ball turret."

"Tail turret."

And then they came. A lone Fortress, obviously in trouble with its bomb bay doors open, was a sitting duck. Two of the hundred-odd ME-109s that had attacked us earlier had followed us out over the North Sea and thought they had us bagged. I could take no evasive action; could only fly straight, slowly letting down. From this stable platform eleven of our .50s chattered, manned by "the best damned crew in the ETO" according to their pilot. After three passes the 109s decided to break it off. Perhaps they were low on fuel. In the brief exchange we had taken a few holes. But, as if in answer to my prayers, none were in the bomb bay and we were still flying steadily. However, I wasn't sure about the crew.

"Crew from copilot," I called. "Check in."

There was no word from the ball turret. He must have been hit. "Waist gunners, check the ball turret."

There was a long period of silence on the interphone while I held my breath. Then Glen Carter, the left waist gunner, reported: "The ball turret gunner's oxygen mask froze. We pulled him out and he's coming around okay. But we ran out of oxygen in the walk-around bottles and I passed out. We're all hooked into the main system now."

Indeed it was "the best damned crew in the ETO," for they not only knew how to fight but how to look after each other. "Good work," I responded. "Keep your eyes peeled. There may be more enemy fighters lurking around. We aren't home yet."

I tried to sound encouraging, but didn't feel that way. A slight air bump could end our lives in a blaze of glory. I concentrated on flying that Fort as never before, each control eased delicately with deliberate precision. Time dragged as we slowly descended. I could almost feel the tension mounting in the crew, but perhaps it was a reflection of my own fear.

We were down to 2,000 feet when I sensed a slight bump. Then Lieutenant Parmer whooped. "It dropped! It's gone!"

The interphone erupted with yells and cries of joy and relief. The fear drained out of us. We were going to live after all.

Sig Thompson took the wheel. "Bomb bay doors closed," he ordered, and navigator Tony Nilo in the nose tripped the lever. Then Sig jammed the throttles forward.

It had been a rough mission for everyone. We had lost four Forts to flak and fighters. I still wasn't truly "blooded," but this mission helped to lessen some of the resentment against me. I knew I would still have to fly many more raids and come home from some with punctured aircraft before being accepted into this very exclusive fraternity, the 384th Bomb Group. But that hung bomb adventure was a beginning.

7

Runaway Prop

Listening to talk at the club bar, I learned that anyone who hadn't flown on a Schweinfurt mission or to Villacoublay or hadn't participated in other bruising 384th battles just wasn't worth associating with. My three missions meant almost nothing. I was still an outsider with no real combat experience, and I found it hard to engage anyone in a conversation.

And, you know, I could hardly blame them. Two years of B-17 flying hadn't prepared me for this new ball game at all. I was a raw recruit, yet it was now my duty to lead the 384th. When something went wrong in the air, as always seemed to happen, it was up to the leader to make the command decisions that would get the formation out of trouble. Was I up to that? Would my decisions be right?

I knew that at the very least I would have to fly several more missions with the 384th before I could win their respect—a conclusion that I wasn't too enthusiastic about, but that was inescapable nonetheless. So three days later, on November 29, 1943, I flew again to Germany.

Bitter cold and wet weather were closing in on Europe, and there were hardly any days now when visual bombing was possible. But to keep the cutting edge of the sword sharp, the Eighth

Air Force was experimenting with blind bombing techniques, and was punching through clouds to Germany in god-awful weather.

The frag order (fragment of the Field Order) that came over the teletype sent us to Bremen again, and the trip nearly ended my career. It wasn't the enemy action that had me reciting my prayers, it was the cold. The weather was even worse than on the previous Bremen mission. Layer upon layer of heavy dark clouds covered the North Sea and Germany.

I hadn't yet picked my own crew. I wanted to fly with each lead crew to see how they performed. The lead crews were the most experienced ones, made up of those who had good records. They were the crews who led our group, or even the combat wing or division, when the 384th was given the honor of leading those larger formations.

The crew I flew with on this mission was headed by Capt. Philip Algar, a cool and thoroughly experienced pilot. We had no blind bombing equipment, so a radar-equipped B-17 had flown up from Alconbury to do the aiming job. It would take over the lead at the Initial Point (IP), and all the rest of us would drop bombs on his signal: six red flares. The Alconbury ship used Oboe blind bombing equipment. It wasn't much good, and records show that this blind bombing seldom hit a target. Nevertheless, we were getting experience.

I sat in the copilot's seat and concentrated on the task of forming into group and wing combat box formations. Luckily our group was in pretty good shape and heading east toward the North Sea before we encountered the heavy weather. But other groups were having trouble. The leader of a group of eighteen that was to form below us in the combat wing formation had misjudged his altitude, and I saw him swinging toward us at our own level. There was nothing I could do but hold my breath during the seconds before his Forts knifed through my formation. One of his B-17s struck one of mine and both went down.

Only luck saved us from other collisions. The 384th must be snake-bit, I thought. Here we had lost a Fort even before we had crossed the enemy coast. On returning from that mission I phoned the group commander involved, and the leader who had made this tragic error never flew again as a pilot.

As our heavily laden Forts droned ahead in the slow climb toward the ominous sky, I witnessed still another tragedy that has since given me nightmares. Far off to the left another combat wing of fifty-four aircraft was attempting to form in the LeMay box formation we used for penetrating Fortress Europe. The lead group over there was higher than we were, and much too near the threatening grey clouds above. I saw that the high group could never join the lead group without forcing its six-ship-high squadron into the freezing overcast. As the high group closed into position, sure enough, its high squadron vanished into the dangerous soup.

B-17s didn't attempt to hold formation in thick weather. Sometimes the mist was so heavy that a pilot could hardly see his own wingtips. Leaders avoided such hazards if they could, but if caught by surprise, as with that high squadron yonder, the SOP was to open up the formation and fly on instruments very accurately straight ahead, praying not to collide with another Fort.

A frightening drama unfolded as I watched that other combat wing far to my left. Two big Forts came hurtling down out of the clouds, spinning wildly. They spun down toward the cold North Sea until I could see them no more. I hoped they would recover from the sickening dive, but Capt. Gordon Stallings, flying in the tail gunner's position to help me control the wing and spot those birds that didn't hold a tight formation, reported seeing no chutes.

At first I suspected a collision, as had happened to us, but on second thought I knew it had to be clear ice. Neither plane seemed to be damaged. No doubt each pilot thought he could regain control, and thus never ordered a bailout.

I had studied the phenomenon of clear ice and knew how

insidious it could be. Under atmospheric conditions of high humidity and freezing temperatures, clear ice could build up on airplane surfaces so rapidly that almost within seconds the craft became too heavy to fly. When this happened there was no recovery. The only answer to clear ice, even today, is to avoid the clouds that cause this deadly condition.

B-17s came to the European Theater of Operations, the ETO, with deicer boots on the leading edges of their wings. The boots would inflate and crack off rime ice, which built up like a white frost to disturb the airflow and lift of the wings. This was the kind of ice that Van Eeuwen and I had encountered over the Rocky Mountains before the war. Rime ice was visible and accumulated slowly, so that a pilot had time to seek a more hospitable altitude. But clear ice was something else again, and the boots were of little help. So to save weight the deicer boots had been stripped from the Forts that were flying combat.

I found a valley in the clouds ahead of us and headed toward it. This gave us space to climb slowly above the overcast without squeezing any of my Forts into the cruel clouds. A fifty-four-plane formation was the most unwieldy and sluggish gaggle of aircraft that one could imagine. Turns, climbs, letdowns, and changes of airspeed had to be made slowly, with infinite care and in minute increments, or the formation would tend to unravel. It was frustrating when a cloud bank had to be avoided. Hazards had to be recognized far in advance and decisions made early. It required from ten to fifteen minutes to turn one of those massive formations around, and the space of many square miles.

The outside temperature dropped to minus 60 degrees Fahrenheit—as low as our thermometer read. I shivered and almost twisted off the rheostats of my electrically heated clothes. I knew if my personal electrical system failed I would quickly freeze, because I couldn't wear a bulky, fleece-lined winter flying suit over my 220-pound frame. Sometimes the side window was the only unobstructed exit from the cockpit of a B-17 headed for Mother Earth. I had seen a pilot leave that way, and I knew my body would never get through that narrow opening if I wore one of those winter flying suits. Moreover, I'd have to hold the belly chute by its handle and hook it on while I fell. But I couldn't find an electrical union suit to fit properly. The one I wore ended at mid-calf, and from there to my boot only the summer flying suit protected my long legs. Now I could feel that part of my anatomy tingling.

Philip Algar's crew suffered in silence. We were all on oxygen, and the ship had shuddered like a dog shaking wet fur when eleven guns had been test-fired. I wondered how those big Wright Cyclone engines could continue their comforting roar in such numbing cold. Soon I began to hear foreign noises. The treacherous clouds built up below us and by the time we reached bombing altitude of 20,000 feet, we were just on top of that dirty, sinister scud. Now I knew that our engines were running rough—all four of them. Captain Algar and I exchanged helpless looks.

When the navigator reported that we were over Bremen I knew he had done a good job, because flak came up through the undercast and burst all around us. The Germans were a good deal more accurate with their radar-directed antiaircraft fire than we were with our blind bombing. Along with the puffs of 88-mm fire that looked like little black men, we were getting larger-caliber stuff that exploded with great red balls of fire.

I signaled for the radar ship to take the lead, and to help settle my churning stomach I grabbed the wheel from Captain Algar and concentrated on flying a close formation with the radar plane. There was one advantage to the mission. Enemy fighters made no attempt to penetrate the icing clouds below us. Our only enemies were cold and flak.

It took an eternity for the radar ship to drop its bombs but finally they fell, along with the red flares, and we were happy to let our bombs go, too. Everyone breathed easier as Philip Algar retook the lead and turned away from the bumping flak that sometimes peppered our ship with shell fragments. But our troubles weren't over.

Number four engine, the outside one on the right, was acting up. We weren't getting much power from it and the other three were operating below par. Then with a terrible scream and whine the prop on number four ran away. RPM shot up past the red line.

I jerked back on the prop control and punched the red feathering button, but the prop wouldn't feather and continued to windmill dangerously. If it twisted off it could cut us to pieces. Even with maximum settings on the other engines we began to lose speed. Pilots following our aircraft were complaining. Some were near to stalling out. As our speed continued to fall off I turned over the lead to the deputy wing leader and Captain Algar left the formation.

It was no fun being alone in that inhospitable sky. Just below was that icing undercast, reaching out with its wispy tendrils to enfold us in a frigid embrace. We were again over the North Sea, and I had visions of clear ice carrying us down into that wet graveyard. We couldn't hold altitude, and continued to sink toward the ominous soup.

Number four engine was still running, but the constant-speed prop control was kaput. Whenever I pushed the control to a higher RPM, the prop would grind up with a deafening roar and threaten to spin off the engine. Still, we were getting some manual control of the prop by jockeying the handle back and forth. A little power was salvaged. By doing this we just managed to stay above the treacherous undercast, and Captain Algar was able to hold enough altitude to clear the lower cloud deck until it ended and we came in sight of England.

Our navigator found an RAF airfield on the coast and Algar greased the crippled Fort into a graceful landing. I soon learned that all of our Forts had returned except the one lost in the collision. But our joy at being safe on terra firma was marred when we learned that a ball turret gunner, Sergeant Kuapa, was dead. He had vomited in his oxygen mask and the vomit had quickly frozen, suffocating him. There was no way he could have called for help.

Unfortunately that mission to Bremen didn't help my standing with the group. My inexperience was rumored as the cause of the midair collision and the loss of a crew, while the slow lead on the way home, along with having to relinquish command, only diminished my sinking reputation further. There was nothing I could have done to avoid that collision, but I supposed there were some people in the group who were glad to hang it on me.

Having spent those weeks with Willie Hatcher's excellent group I found many things about the 384th that I didn't like. Discipline was poor from top to bottom. People slopped around in disheveled uniforms of every description. No one saluted. The station was a quagmire of mud. In fact, it was referred to throughout the Eighth as Grafton Undermud. And instead of attempting to get rid of the mud, the troops seemed to use the mud as an excuse for their sloppy behavior.

I came to the conclusion that I couldn't wait to gain some sort of popularity and respect before taking drastic action to whip this group into shape. We were losing too many airplanes and having excessive aborts—crews that returned before ever crossing the channel. Most of the aborts were legitimate since maintenance of aircraft was lousy, as illustrated by our runaway prop. Defects and engine troubles usually appeared shortly after takeoff, whereupon pilots would abort the mission and return to Grafton.

I could no longer contain the many plans I had in mind that needed to be carried out, but I approached the task gingerly at first. I was beginning to despair of ever winning their confidence through friendly overtures or persuasion. My only recourse seemed to be an arbitrary command, the iron fist. The situation had become so critical that I resolved to force the reforms on the group if need be.

One of the outstanding deficiencies was a lack of teamwork and precision. Each of the four squadron commanders was at swords' points with the others, and in addition each considered the group headquarters itself an unnecessary echelon of command. With some justification, everyone blamed Engineering for the excessive aborts. Staff meetings were bitterly acrimonious, and I struggled helplessly to gain some spirit of cooperation. This attitude was mirrored in the group's air work. Formations were ragged, squadrons didn't support each other, flight plans were haphazardly followed, and leadership was often ignored. Radio frequencies crackled with morbid humor and irritated profanity. There was no way to tell who was cluttering up the transmissions. Takeoffs were sluggish, drawn-out affairs.

I began the buck-up program with the takeoff technique. The merits of a snappy takeoff procedure were not readily apparent to people of the 384th. No one seemed to feel that anything was to be gained by starting all engines at the same instant, by having all airplanes begin to taxi to their takeoff positions on the exact second, or by each bomber roaring into the air at precise thirty-second intervals. Ample time was always allowed for late takeoffs to join the formation in the air, and there were frequently genuine troubles that caused delays.

On the other hand, with precise takeoffs a feeling of integrity and strength could be developed. When several hundred people in massive warplanes moved together as a well-oiled machine, with none faltering, none jamming the works, and everyone able to depend on everyone else, mutual confidence was gained. I had felt it in other groups, and I knew that such a spirit of unity would carry over into the air work, where everything counted so dearly.

I had become aware of the tense, dreadful wait in the airplanes after "stations" (when the crews were in place) and before "start engines." If pyrotechnics were used to signal the various takeoff activities, the distraction might tend to ease the anxiety. Such a system, which required no additional work from anyone except the flare shooter, might become popular. Moreover, the idea was made to order for the opening wedge of the many reforms I had in mind.

At the next staff meeting I suggested the new procedure. "Gentlemen, I've been thinking how we might put a little more color and zip into our takeoffs. We have varicolored flares. I saw another outfit use flares to signal the times to start engines, taxi, and take off. It looked pretty impressive and the crews seemed to get a kick out of it. I know we calibrate watches at briefings and everyone knows the exact second to start engines, and so forth, but flares will remind those not looking at their watches. On top of that, it might encourage the pilots to move off together. What do you think?"

I could count on general disapproval, but was sure that a verbal objection would come from the commander of the 544th Squadron, Lt. Col. Alfred Nuttall, and it did. Nuttall was considered one of our best leaders, but his constant negativism annoyed me. "Can't see that it does anything more than to add extra duties for someone to fire the flares," he said. "I think they move off together okay now. Only reason some might not is because of a mechanical problem. Flares wouldn't make any difference there."

"It might cause a little extra work," I agreed, "but hardly enough to wear anyone out." I wanted to avoid the touchy subject of precision. I knew they were thinking *he wants to drill us like West Pointers*. It was obvious that my standards of precision were considerably higher than those of the staff, and I didn't want to get involved in a futile argument. I realized that my remark was a mistake because it held an element of sarcasm not conducive to persuasion, but I had to let it hang.

"Well," said Nuttall, "one of the busiest men on takeoffs is the flying control officer. If we add even a little job like flare shooting to his list of duties, he's likely to make a mistake in recording the takeoffs or something else. He's plenty busy. Did you ever watch him?"

I ignored the implication that I didn't know what went on in the control tower. I couldn't allow Nuttall to trick me into an argument unrelated to the issue, particularly when such an argument would involve my defending myself before the whole staff. I was ready for the too-much-work objection, however.

"The group navigator gives the time hacks at briefings," I noted. "He's the man who keeps all the clocks on the right second. What does he do after briefings?"

Nuttall was unprepared for that question. "Goes to bed, I guess," he said.

"Any reason why he can't fire the flares?" I asked.

"No, I guess not." But Nuttall had recovered with a new objection. "I don't like it though, Colonel. If everyone gets used to flares they won't pay any attention to their watches. Then one day the flare shooter won't turn up and the whole group will get off late."

"I suppose that could happen," I said, "but we won't make any change in existing instructions. We could just superimpose the flare shooting onto our regular takeoff sop. Just tell people that flares are an additional reminder. As for the flare shooter, we'd have to depend on him. In this business there are many individuals we have to depend on. You know that."

"Seems to me we already have enough details to worry about," grumbled Nuttall, "without dreaming up more that we could get along without."

I sensed that he was running out of specific objections and that the others who had taken no sides were ready at least to close the subject and get on with more pressing matters. Then I gave them the needle. It went in so gently that they never realized it was the beginning of an injection that would revolutionize the outfit.

"Well, suppose we give it a try," I said. "Let's work it a while, and if you don't like it we'll cut it out." This was an arbitrary order and they knew it. Discussion was closed. I hadn't gained their support, or even their grudging consent; all I had done was to take some of the venom from their objections. By now I knew that any suggestion I might voice would be rejected on general principles. But if this takeoff plan worked, my next suggestion might be given more consideration on its basic merits.

Nuttall and the others agreed with the reservations, and the program for precision takeoffs was inaugurated as a standing operating procedure, an SOP.

In the early morning darkness before the next combat mission, twenty-two crews watched the control tower as their second hands crept to "start engines" time. Energizers were meshed ten seconds before, and when the two yellow flares burst above the control tower, twenty-two engines coughed into thundering life. These were quickly followed by the starting of the other sixty-six engines, and in a moment the airfield was throbbing with their roar of power. We were putting up a group of eighteen with four spares. If no more than four aborted the mission the spares would fill in, so that we would go to war with a full complement of eighteen Forts, as called for in the frag order from Division.

Five minutes later green and yellow flares exploded in the darkness. The lumbering bombers began to move as a single unit, jockeying for position on the concrete taxiways circling the airfield to their takeoff position at the end of the mile-long runway. Then the final green-green flare signaled the leading Fortress to give it the gun and it rolled down the runway, shooting flames from its four exhaust stacks, picking up speed, and lifting into the air just before reaching the end of the runway. This was followed by another and another and another, at exactly thirty-second intervals, until all twenty-two were airborne and making the world tremble with their thundering vibrations as they circled above the field. It was the best takeoff in the group's history. Nothing had been changed. Only some color and interest had been added.

At the next staff conference Nuttall volunteered the information that the crews liked the flares and that perhaps we might as well continue with the custom. The group navigators even enjoyed shooting the flares with the Very pistol. It was sort of like pulling the trigger that set the several-hundred-thousand-horsepower juggernaut in motion. I thanked Nuttall for his help in getting the procedure under way and turned the discussion to flares in general.

"No reason why we can't use them more," I said. "The armament officer tells me we have a warehouse full of them."

"Well," suggested the air exec Willie Buck, "the leader fires them for self-identification to help his wing men form on him."

I knew I had hit the jackpot. This practice of periodic firing of flares was useless. In a large gaggle of B-17s milling around a radio beacon as I had witnessed on the Knaben mission, all looked alike, and finding one's leader was usually impossible. Even if a pilot saw flares fired he'd usually lose track of the leader among the dozens of other Forts. I suspected flares would have to be fired one after another as fast as possible, so that a continual stream of flares would be issuing from the leader.

"Yes," I said, "but when you look for a leader he isn't firing flares, and when someone in your plane sees flares, by the time he calls you the flares are out and all you see is two trails of smoke where the leader was a few moments ago."

"Yeah," broke in Lt. Col. Tom Beckett, the operations officer, "it doesn't work too well. Can't see the colors half the time and so you don't know what leader it might be."

"How often does the leader fire flares?" I asked.

"Every few seconds," someone said.

"I guess they could be fired oftener," Willie suggested.

"A swell idea," I jumped in. "The engineer does the shooting. Why doesn't he fire one after the other as fast as he can? Then maybe the wing men could identify their leader better."

"Worth a try," said Willie. "Sure use up a lot of flares, though."

"You have my full authority to use all the flares you can fire," I said. "If you decide it helps forming up let me know and we'll get out an SOP on it."

The ice was broken somewhat. Before long Nuttall became a supporter of my proposals and Willie Buck and Tom Beckett reluctantly followed. But it was the ground exec, Lt. Col. James Taff, who suffered the brunt of my buck-up program. When things moved too slowly I leaned on him pretty heavily.

There was still no word from Elise. My emotions were so strained that I needed the warmth of her letters. The yearning for mail became almost physical in its intensity. I wrote:

> My dearest,
>
> Still no word from you and I pester the post office every day but they give me no answers. I must have confused you by giving you so many APO numbers, but now my APO won't change and mail should reach me here. Please be sure to use the number on this letter. Any other number will cause the mail to go astray and end up Lord knows where.
>
> This group is a great fighting unit and I feel lucky to have landed such an assignment. I've been on two missions with them and they've deported themselves with honor. The danger isn't nearly as great as the newspapers make it out to be and I know I'll get home to you when it's all over.

I miss you terribly, Sweetheart, and dream of you almost every night. How I wish I could spend just an hour with you and the kids. It would give me new resolve to carry on. I get so lonely over here, so far from you. Please write. Your letters are precious.

The other day as I was driving through a small English village I saw a small boy and girl playing in a school yard. I wanted to stop and talk with them, they reminded me so of Kort and Voan. This childless and womanless environment is not my idea of living.

I love you, dear, and when this is all over I know we can make a good life for ourselves and our kids. Don't get discouraged. It won't last forever.

Much, much love

Dale

8

The Duke and I

I wore high overshoes when I took command at Grafton Underwood from Con Lacey. Station 106 certainly deserved its pejorative sobriquet of Grafton Under*mud*. It wasn't located in a bog, but the clay soil held the frequent rains and the place was a sea of sticky brown muck.

It was irritating and depressing. Everyone slogged to the mess halls—we had four of them—in caked overshoes, parking them inside the doors, but mud somehow invaded every building and dried on the floors. When we left, all about the same time, it was an irascible scramble to find one's own overshoes. Many men ended up with overshoes that didn't fit. It was a situation hardly conducive to good morale.

Tires of the five-ton trucks that plied the roads on group business dripped with mire. Mud was tracked onto the taxiways and hardstands where the B-17s were parked, and accumulated on their wheels. There were instances of landing gear sticking in the up position when the mud froze. Something had to be done and soon.

One day I dug down in the mud on our roads and discovered that under the mud was a lane of concrete pavement, with occasional concrete turnouts for passing. We began to shovel the mud off the pavement. There were miles of roads, but we had thousands of people. Almost everyone, with my persuasion, did his bit with a shovel. They grumbled, but they shoveled, and the roads slowly began to clear. I put out orders that trucks were henceforth to stay on the pavement and pass only at the concrete turnouts.

One morning as I walked from my quarters to the Officers' Mess I witnessed two trucks approaching head-on. One swung off the pavement into the mud to pass. I stopped it and confronted the driver, a buck sergeant. Had he seen my directive about passing? He had. Why did he then drive off the pavement? He was in a hurry to deliver some supplies and didn't want to waste time by backing to a turnout. I took his name and outfit.

That morning I called his squadron commander—I think it was Nuttall—and told him to bust the sergeant to private as an example, then, after an appropriate time, to promote him back to his original grade. My action was roundly condemned by everyone (of course Nuttall was enjoined to make no mention of the fact that the sergeant's rank would later be restored). My popularity sank to a new low, if that were possible. It was draconian punishment for such a minor offense, but they got the message. Trucks stayed on the concrete.

The roads finally cleared, and I congratulated myself for the success of the campaign. Morale was improving and people could walk the roads without overshoes. Bicycles appeared, along with smiles and a few more salutes. Then one morning as I walked to work I was shocked to find the roads once again deep in mud. Where had it come from? And how could it accumulate so fast?

Surveying the base in my beat-up staff car I found a huge dump truck loaded with muck, oozing mud onto its caked double wheels and thence to the road. It wasn't a military vehicle. Where had it come from and where was it going? I followed it to a field where it dumped its load and then to another field near our hangar where a large power shovel loaded it with more mud from a mound. There were several such dump trucks, and each traversed the base from end to end. It hadn't taken long to undo weeks of labor and again leave Grafton Under*mud*.

I immediately called my ground exec, Lieutenant Colonel Taff. Yes, he knew all about it but could do nothing. The mud movers were working for the Duke of Buccleuch, who owned our base. I learned that we were paying him rent of thirty thousand dollars a month for the spread.

"Okay," I said, "let's call the Duke and politely ask him to cease and desist." Moving mud from one field to another didn't seem to be a high-priority effort during a hot war.

Colonel Taff had already tried that, he said, to no avail. So I tried the phone but didn't get the Duke. His manager reported that His Excellency was "shooting in Scotland." I requested the manager to stop the mud-hauling trucks but he could do nothing, he said, without the Duke's approval. I didn't like his manner. He showed no concern for our problem. In fact, he was rather curt and certainly uncooperative. I gathered that the war was a dreadful bore to him, particularly with those Yanks everywhere.

This thoroughly annoyed me, and I instructed Taff to put guards on the gates to those mud fields and not let a single one of the Duke's trucks pass.

Within hours all hell broke loose. High-ranking Brits from the Air Ministry in London called me; the Duke was a member of the royal family. Generals from Eighth Air Force Headquarters admonished me. I couldn't do that, they told me. The rental agreement allowed the Duke to use our roads. I was hindering good relations with our British allies, etc.

I told my immediate administrative boss, Bob Williams, that as long as I was in command there would be no more mud tracked on our roads and that if he wanted this order changed he would have to relieve me of command. He took this insubordination with his usual good grace, and as the days went by without my receiving transfer orders I realized he had gone to bat for me in his talks with the Olympian powers in London.

Again the roads of Grafton Underwood cleared, while the Duke's trucks and power shovel remained dead in the fields. They were still there when I departed the station eleven months later. Needless to say, the Duke never returned my call, and never visited our Station 106.

The 384th flew ten missions in December in weather that made sensible ducks stay home. Freezing temperatures, layers of black clouds, drizzling rain, and sleet were our usual fare. On December 1 Maj. Maurice A. Dillingham, commanding the 547th Squadron, led the raid to Solingen, in the German Ruhr. It was a rugged one, and Dillingham was shot down. I had judged him one of the best squadron commanders, whom I had counted on to help me buck up the group, and I felt his loss keenly. In his place I appointed Capt. Horace A. Frink, Jr., a skillful pilot and perhaps the bravest man in the group, who seemed to have no fear whatever of flak or fighters. He became a superb combat leader, and his new position soon gained him the rank of major.

On December 5 Lt. Col. Tom Beckett, our operations officer, led the raid to La Rochelle, France, but he had to abort the mission because of the bad weather. On the eleventh Maj. Raymond P. Ketelsen, who commanded the 545th Squadron, led a successful raid on targets near Emden and returned with no losses. On the thirteenth Gen. Bob Travis, our combat wing commander, sent Colonel Romig, one of his staff officers, to lead another Bremen mission. He flew with Nuttall's crew. It was another inconclusive blind bombing operation. I led again on the sixteenth with Capt. Edgar Ulrey's crew. It was still another Bremen raid, and I was getting tired of flying there. Willie Buck led another effort toward Bremen on the twentieth, but the weather turned him back. He led again on the twenty-second to bomb the Osnabrück marshaling yards, and still again on a blind bombing raid to Ludwigshafen in the German Ruhr on December 30. I don't know why it was that Willie volunteered to lead so many missions in December. Perhaps he was trying to quickly accumulate the twenty-five missions that would end his combat tour. Ketelsen again led a mission on the twenty-fourth to bomb marshaling yards at Croixette, France.

The last day of 1943 dawned with the usual thick overcast and a weeping sky. We had been promised a "stand-down" by Division, and I planned a New Year's celebration for all hands. They had been working awfully hard under my whip, but were making real progress and everyone certainly deserved a chance to cut loose. But our promised stand-down went up in smoke when we got a frag order to seek out and destroy a German blockade runner in the mouth of the Garonne River in southwestern France.

Horace Frink took off at dawn, leading our group of eighteen birds, but he was unable to find the blockade runner—bad weather again—and returned late in the afternoon when darkness was falling. He found England almost entirely socked in. It had been a nine-hour mission and all the B-17s were short of fuel. I had nightmare visions of losing the whole group in crash landings and bailouts. Why hadn't Division recalled them when their weather people saw that the whole island was closing in? All this for a lousy blockade runner.

With my weather officer I scanned the maps of England making calls and searching for airfields where our birds might land. None looked favorable. Division was doing the same thing, and between us we managed to divert fifteen into fields with marginal weather. But Grafton Underwood was deep in darkening fog. Perhaps we had 100 feet of ceiling, with visibility no more than a quarter of a mile.

I was on the roof of our control tower with mike and earphones tuned to the command frequency when I heard the drone of one of our Forts somewhere in the overcast above. He had arrived over the field after homing on our radio beacon, which we called a "splasher." By that time I had set out sodium vapor landing flares at the upwind end of the active north-south runway and was lining the runway with more flares. These flares were stowed like cordwood in a ground-floor room of the control tower, and I urged the men to hurry it up and set out more and more of them. They scurried like ants attacking a sugar cube as they loaded the flares into trucks and sped to the runway.

"Grafton this is Clinker H for Harry. Landing instructions."

"Hello Clinker H. This is Colonel Smith. The field is socked in. About a hundred feet and a quarter mile. Do you see the landing flares?"

"Negative."

"What is your altitude?"

"One thousand."

"Okay, home on the splasher and then turn South for two minutes. Then make a one-eighty and home on the splasher again. When you hit the splasher turn to sixty degrees for four minutes and let down to five hundred feet. You'll be on the downwind leg. Then make a half-needle turn of one-eighty to your left. Now you should be on the final at two-forty degrees. Let down at one hundred feet per minute to one hundred feet. When you see the flares land toward them. Never mind hitting the runway. You get all that?"

"Roger." He didn't sound very confident. There was a hint of panic in his voice. I decided to keep on talking.

"Just fly out a short distance from the splasher south, and then make a one-eighty back to it. Okay?"

"Okay."

"Then when you hit the splasher turn to sixty degrees immediately. I know you can do it." There was no answer. I could see him concentrating on his instruments.

Then another call came in: "Grafton this is Dragoon D for dog. How's the weather?"

"Not good, Dragoon D, but there's nowhere else to go. Call me when you hit the splasher."

Now I could hear Clinker H's engines over the splasher and turning to 60 degrees. "You're doing fine, Clinker H. I hear you. Remember, turn to sixty degrees on the downwind and let down to five hundred feet."

"Dragoon D over the splasher," came the call. I repeated the instructions I had given Clinker H and then another and still another distressed bird called in. I was having trouble keeping track of them and depended on the engine noise overhead. Then some clumsy airman carrying flares out of the control tower dropped an armful and somehow managed to pull the igniting wire. Instantly the tower became engulfed in flame and smoke. The fire trucks were on it immediately but they made so much noise I couldn't hear the bomber engines above in the overcast. I called down to the firemen: "Shut off those goddam engines!" I didn't care if the tower burned down as long as I got those Forts on the ground. It didn't occur to me that if the tower burned down I'd go with it. Dutifully the fire engines became quiet, but they had doused the worst of the flames and were using hand extinguishers to finish the job.

About that time Clinker H emerged from the clouds. He was somewhat left of the runway, high and fast, but he managed to set his Fort down and roll to a safe stop at the end of the field. Right behind him came Dragoon D. He was short, but he gunned his engines and bounced to another safe stop. The next two were almost out of gas and it was getting darker. The pilots were so wound up they couldn't concentrate. They might run out of gas on the letdown or otherwise crash. I told them to head toward The Wash, set their automatic pilots so their B-17s would fly out to sea, and bail out.

There wasn't anything else I could do, so I headed for the

Officers' Club where one of the New Year's parties was in session. I needed a drink.

Just before midnight I received a call from Operations that all of the crewmen who had bailed out were accounted for. None were injured. We hadn't lost a man on this terrifying snafu. At midnight of the New Year I reported this news to all personnel. Spirits rose with loud cheers. It was going to be a good year for the 384th after all. I knew it.

9

Lieutenant Jacobs's Example

The 384th had an unenviable record of aborts. We ranked somewhere near the bottom of all the VIII Bomber Command groups. Bob Travis, the ambitious brigadier general who commanded the 41st Combat Wing under which we suffered, hammered on me frequently to do something about our miserable record. Every now and then he'd send one of his bright staff officers to Grafton Underwood to instruct us on how to handle the problem.

I thought I knew why we had so many aborts. It was simply a consequence of our overall low morale. Admittedly our maintenance wasn't too hot. Other groups—there were about twenty-five B-17 groups in the VIII Bomber Command at that time—suffered equal hardships. But we seemed to have more mechanical failures than the others.

The ground pounders in our group, however, were treated like second-class citizens, particularly the men of the Sub Depot, which was created under the command of Maj. John H. Humphries about the time I arrived. They had their own mess, separate from the mess of the elite extra-paid air crews. It was located off in the woods about a mile from the central communal area where the large Quonset containing the "Little Foxy Theater" stood, along with other temporary buildings housing the Combat Crew Mess, the Officers' Mess, and the Service Club run by two hard-working Red Cross girls. The very location of the Ground Crew Mess separated them from the mainstream of the group. Seldom did a member of the maintenance and supply echelon receive any recognition for the backbreaking work performed under adverse conditions. Much of the aircraft repair had to be done at night, in the open, hampered by winter rain or snow. And, of course, the Ordnance squadron had to load bombs after midnight, when the frag order established the details of the mission and the bomb load.

So one of my first "reforms" was to integrate the messes. There would be no distinction made between ground and air personnel. We would be a unified team, cooperating with and depending on one another at all times. I also instructed Taff to look for ways to recognize individuals in the ground echelon who did outstanding work. They too deserved Good Conduct Medals and letters of commendation.

The airmen's Combat Crew Mess became the Airmen's Mess, feeding all personnel of the first three grades: privates, corporals, and buck sergeants. The Ground Crew Mess now catered to all staff, technical, and master sergeants, and became the NCO Mess. I authorized the NCOs to remodel a building nearby that had once been a Royal Air Force NAFE outlet, a store for necessities similar to our Post Exchange. This building became the "Zebra Club" (lots of stripes) for all the senior noncommissioned officers. I was honored to be invited to the grand opening.

Remembering the maxim of Napoléon that an army marches on its stomach, I decided to do something about the food that was being served. It was pure hash-house fare in the Officers' Mess, the poor quality being blamed on the rations provided. I hardly had the courage to finish a meal. I ate meals at the new Airmen's and NCO messes and found them even worse. How come Willie Hatcher had such a fine mess and we didn't? We received the same, identical rations as the Polebrook outfit.

To begin with I sent a cook from each mess to Polebrook on

temporary duty, to find out how Willie's messes operated. They returned full of ideas and enthusiasm. One remarkable discovery (I'm not sure whether it came from Polebrook; it might have been discovered at Grafton) was that the stinking powdered eggs and powdered milk could be made palatable. There were tons of this powder available in the Commissary, because no one in the Eighth Air Force could stomach the stuff. One of our enterprising cooks found that by mixing the powder and water with a high-speed electric beater for twenty-four hours, the eggs and milk lost their offensive odor and began to taste like the fresh articles. Mixing the two together with sugar and seasoning created delicious eggnogs, and adding powdered chocolate made a delightful chocolate milk drink. We kept large pitchers of these drinks on the tables at all times, and they were frequently refilled.

But before this could happen we had to find a way to mix great quantities of these drinks. This problem was solved when the Sub Depot rigged mixers run by B-17 starter motors, which ran continuously, night and day, in large vats of the mixture. We found, too, that delicious omelets and pastries could be made with the treated eggs. Fresh eggs were rare and precious, and were served only to combat crews who were scheduled on a mission.

The British food ration had considerably less variety than that provided to the American forces, yet I noted that London hotels managed to turn out quite tasty dishes. So Taff, caught in the spirit of reform, sent three of our top cooks on temporary duty to London, with instructions to study techniques of the best London chefs. There was a noticeable improvement in the meals on their return. Moreover, those cooks and mess sergeants who discovered better ways to prepare and serve meals were beginning to be recognized with awards and decorations.

An enterprising mess officer found an ice cream factory in Kettering that had been forced to shut down. With Officers' Club funds we bought the factory and moved it to our station.

Using our unlimited supply of powdered milk and eggs, we produced tons of delicious ice cream, even serving free ice cream cones in the Foxy Theater to all comers.

After a while I was pleased to find people from other groups dropping in to eat in one of our messes. And when I asked an airman why he had returned early from leave he told me he got tired of London food and wanted to get home for a good meal.

While all this was going on, I was knocking myself out to find ways to reduce our unsatisfactory abort rate. I suspected that not all the aborts were because of mechanical failures; some of the pilots were imagining troubles, or were returning because of troubles that were not serious enough to warrant an abort. Certain pilots seemed to abort more often than others, and I intended to find out why.

One of these pilots was 2nd Lt. Randolph Jacobs. After being badly mauled on the mission to Ludwigshafen in the Ruhr on December 30, he ditched in the Channel and one of his crew drowned leaving the broken bomber. Jacobs and the others were rescued by a Royal Navy coastal patrol boat. I could understand that he might have been a little overcautious.

On a mission to Kiel on January 4, Jacobs had aborted, reporting engine trouble. Lt. Col. Tom Beckett, my Ops officer, told me that Jacobs was a repeated offender.

"I think Jacobs is a liar," Beckett said. "He keeps complaining about a rough engine but Engineering says it's okay. He's a loud-mouthed blowhard and no credit to his outfit. Nuttall wants to get him transferred out."

So I decided to call Jacobs on the carpet and make an example of him. This was what my ragged group needed, another example. I was disgusted with those who found questionable excuses not to go to war with us. In the infantry, desertion before the enemy was punishable by death. In the Air Force one could complain of engine trouble or something else and go unpunished.

Big, swarthy Lieutenant Jacobs saluted defiantly and

looked me straight in the eye. Most people called on the carpet before a bird colonel were somewhat intimidated; but not this guy. He seemed to welcome the opportunity.

"Why did you abort?" I demanded.

"My number two engine was rough." He added no "sir" and his harsh voice was insolent.

"I've been told you've used the same excuse twice before," I snapped, "but each time the engine checked out. Engineering reports it's okay now."

"They're wrong!" He almost spit it out. "I asked last time for an engine change and they wouldn't give it to me. That engine's a bag of bolts."

Fighting for control, I got up to stoke the midget coke stove, which usually smoked and seemed to keep my dingy office just above freezing, at best. Jacobs stood at a slouching attention. Could he possibly be telling the truth? But how could all those reports be wrong? Still, under a cloud of doom it's mighty easy to hear a strange engine noise that isn't there. Self-deception isn't the same as cowardice. I stowed the poker and returned to my chair. Arrogant disrespect flashed from his sullen dark eyes, which were crowned by rumpled black hair and separated by a too-ample nose. No, he couldn't be the gutless type. Not that, at least. Cowards don't behave defiantly.

For that matter, I wasn't too confident that Beckett's report was accurate. With four aborts on the mission, who else might be lying? Even if Jacobs were outbluffing me, I had to be more sure of my ground. I couldn't risk any more group antagonism without losing control of the group altogether.

I assumed my most severe manner: "Lieutenant Jacobs," I intoned, "if you abort once more I'm going to have you busted to a flight officer and you'll finish your tour as a copilot; that is, if I can find a pilot who will have you. But I'll give you one last break. Tomorrow we take delivery of a new plane. It's a silver B-17G, the best flying machine America has produced. It's the first to come to us without camouflage paint, and it will stand out among the other mud-colored Fortresses like a new dime among pennies. That will be your ship as long as you fly her honorably."

Jacobs missed the next two missions because the silver B-17G wasn't combat ready. I wondered what was causing the delay and decided to visit Lt. Col. Alfred Nuttall, Jacobs's squadron commander. On the way in the cold rain I noticed two spattered trucks drawn up beside some Quonsets. I could tell one truck was filled with replacement personnel, because of the clean uniforms, and I parked my staff car to look them over. The newcomers sat glumly under the dripping canvas, while a fatigue detail loaded the other truck with poorly packed gear and dirty laundry from the barracks. Then I knew what was happening. The replacements were being moved right into the warm bunks of those who had failed to return from the last operation. This was one hell of a dreary greeting.

An officer in a raincoat stepped up to the truck's tailgate and spoke to the new men. I looked closer. It was Jacobs. He didn't notice my car, which was shielded by the other truck, but I was close enough to hear him.

"Well, boys," he chided, "so the draft finally caught you. I know this place doesn't look like home, but don't worry. You won't be around long. That truck over there is being loaded with all that remains of those brave airmen you're replacing."

That was as much as I could take. I moved the car up and honked, angrily motioning Jacobs to come.

"Climb in," I ordered. He obeyed without comment. "Are you in charge of those new men?" I asked. He shook his head. "That's some morale lecture you gave them. Are you trying to make them flak happy before they fly a mission?"

I stomped on the gas and drove to Jacobs's squadron, where I found Nuttall worrying over a pile of paperwork. With Jacobs waiting outside the cubicle office, I told the harassed squadron commander what I'd witnessed.

"Lieutenant Jacobs," Nuttall sighed, rolling his bloodshot eyes to the ceiling, "is my biggest headache. Colonel, I wish you'd get rid of him. Why, before I can get my replacements to the orientation lecture, Jacobs has filled them with gruesome war stories."

"Do you think it makes him feel important?" I asked.

"Maybe. But his big mouth is ruining the squadron."

"Al, the guy seems tough enough. Can't you find something for him to do where his bragging would help? Like briefing new crews on procedures? Tactics?"

"My God, give him a rostrum to scare the men more?"

"No. Charge him with building up confidence. Then he could boast by showing them what a piece of cake the war is."

"I don't think it'll work. We ought to get rid of him."

"That's not easy," I said. "And it'd set a bad example."

Al Nuttall spread his hands in resignation.

"What about the new aircraft?" I asked.

"Colonel, it was a mistake to assign that to him. That silver job's a sure death trap. You can see it a hundred miles. And Jacobs won't even fly a regular B-17. Besides, the new bird has some instruments missing."

"But Al, you know damn well all of our replacement aircraft are going to be silver Gs from now on. They're hundreds of pounds lighter and faster than the painted jobs."

"We could paint 'em so they wouldn't be so conspicuous."

"We could," I said, "but we aren't going to."

"The instruments it needs aren't in stock," he said. "We've requisitioned them from Bovington but no dice." I knew he was dragging his feet, and maybe he saw my ire rising because he called in Jacobs for verification.

Jacobs almost swaggered as he took the chair Nuttall indicated. Perversely I was glad to see that Jacobs showed his squadron commander no more deference than he had me. Al asked him about the B-17G.

"She'll fly the next mission," Jacobs announced. "She's in commission now."

Nuttall raised his heavy eyebrows.

"I couldn't wait for Supply to get off their duffs," Jacobs continued, "so I went to Bovington on my day off and dug up the instruments myself."

What was this? Was Jacobs the only one in the squadron who wanted the silver bird to fly? He had shown such unusual enterprise that I found myself in a strange alliance with the group oddball. Just to check a hunch I asked Nuttall how Jacobs's old airplane, given to another crew, had fared on the last mission. The squadron commander hesitated only a moment before blurting the embarrassing truth.

"Abort," he said.

"What caused it?" I asked.

"Number two engine failure."

So Jacobs had told the truth! I glanced at him. He was gloating.

Nuttall then lit into Jacobs for scaring the new men, and charged him henceforth with the task of briefing the new crews on the conduct of the war in such a way as to raise morale. Jacobs seemed to like the idea.

It stopped raining that night and we loaded up for Ludwigshafen again. In the briefing theater I noticed Jacobs talking animatedly with some nearby men who were trying hard to ignore him. Later, in the cold dawn outside, I managed to speak to him as he was throwing his parachute aboard the truck that was taking his crew to the hardstand.

"Good luck, Lieutenant," I said.

He regarded me quizzically. I suppose not many people wished Jacobs luck. He managed to say, "Thanks, Colonel."

Operations had carefully positioned Jacobs's silver plane in the center of the formation, where it might not be so much of an attraction. The tail gunner on the lead ship told me that Jacobs never got so much as a foot out of place. For our group, at least, the mission was flown with some success. We hit the rail yards, losing only one Fort, and it wasn't Jacobs's plane. But there were two aborts.

Spring came, and with better weather the tempo of raids increased. Although our loss and abort rates diminished some, the more frequent operations caused the totals to rise sharply. And after twenty-five missions the crews who survived were rotated Stateside. Our most experienced men went home. The 384th couldn't seem to get out from under the bottom of the heap.

I could feel the hot breath of the combat wing commander, Brig. Gen. Bob Travis, on my neck. The group buck-up he had expected from me was not happening as quickly as he liked. Another replacement colonel had been sent to the group "to fly a few missions and get oriented." Was he being groomed to fill my shoes?

Driving out to my Fortress one grey morning I heard that loud penetrating voice and stopped the car on the taxi strip. Jacobs was briefing a crew. The men were huddled around a jeep while Jacobs, his sleeves rolled up, earnestly lectured from the driver's seat. I couldn't hear all he said, but his tone was reassuring and the crew attentive.

"Now don't forget to keep your eyes open for fighters," I heard him warn. "Stay on the ball and I'll see you tonight." Then he was off with a terrible clash of gears and skidding rubber. He drove to the next hardstand, and as the crew there began to tumble out of the Fortress and gather around the jeep, I knew he was repeating the pep talk. This was a new Jacobs.

Perhaps I, too, should give a pep talk, I thought. Maybe I could get volunteers for extra missions and keep some experienced crews. I intended to stay in combat until the end of the war, but I had never told anyone this. I decided to make a public announcement and ask others to join me.

The group gathered in our drafty hangar where I stood on a maintenance platform to make my pitch. Only about a third of the three thousand showed up. I told them how we were winning the war. How much better they were getting. (To an extent it was true, but not much.) How necessary it was to retain our experience. This way we could fight better and suffer fewer losses. Then I told them I intended to keep flying regardless of how many missions it took to whip the Jerries, and I needed some volunteers to help me.

The silence was deafening. My effort was a flat flop. I couldn't have been repudiated more decisively.

That evening I went to the club bar to try to thaw a chill in my bones that was caused from more than the Midlands fog. My ration of Irish whiskey was poured by the amiable Primo, who owned his own bar in Boston and acted here as a father confessor. I wished I could tell him my troubles, and realized how close I was to crying in my beer like so many of the others.

Al Nuttall joined me and I rolled him for the iceless drinks. As I paid the chit he said, "Your idea sure worked about Jacobs. He's my Ops officer now and does the work of three men. And he hasn't aborted since you gave him that first silver Fort."

"Sounds like you want to promote him," I said.

"I do, dammit. And he deserves it."

"So we promote him. He flies a few more missions and goes home. As soon as a man gets good we lose him. It's a treadmill."

"Yeah," said Nuttall, "there's not many of us left who were with old Colonel Peaslee. Those were the days." There was reverence in his tone, and the invidious comparison didn't escape me.

While making aimless rings along the bar with my glass I became conscious of someone standing on the other side of me. Turning, I saw Jacobs. The defiant look was gone. He looked proud. I saw something else, too.

Jacobs was giving me the first look of downright respect

ever tendered me on that station. Suddenly I realized that I liked and respected Jacobs, too, and returned his look.

It occurred to me then that there were many other good, sincere fighting men in the 384th, and that if I could respect Jacobs I could just as well respect them all. Certainly I could ask for no loyalty from them until I extended it.

With a flash of insight I saw the whole situation. I realized why the 384th couldn't climb out of its depression. My approach had been little better than Peaslee's. True, I had given them drills and discipline. They could carry out their assignments pretty well now. But the spirit that would make them champions was missing. I had doubted and distrusted them. But no more. Never again.

I shot my hand out to Jacobs and he grasped it warmly. "Colonel Smith," he said, "this afternoon I heard you ask for more than twenty-five missions."

I nodded.

"Well, I want to volunteer for five more—I'll go thirty."

Another pilot, overhearing Jacobs, stepped forward. "I'll go five more, too, Colonel," he said. Then two more volunteered. I was kept busy buying drinks for volunteers. The ice was broken. The 384th was on its way to the top.

Lieutenant Randolph Jacobs never completed his five extra missions. On his twenty-eighth mission he took a direct flak hit over the Pas de Calais, and no one got out. In war there is no such thing as fair play.

10

The Raid on Kiel

America was beginning to turn out silver B-17Gs like hotcakes. They had forward-shooting chin turrets with two .50s, and we loved them. What's more, the home front was turning out B-17 crews to match the surge of bombers coming off the production lines. There were enough aircraft with crews coming to England to upgrade all the VIII Bomber Command groups. My four squadrons were originally each equipped with nine aircraft and crews. Now each had about a dozen or more, along with extra crews. And this figure continued to rise.

It was a credit to our maintenance people that we could report thirty-six or more planes in commission for combat every day. On January 4, 1944, we were ordered to bomb the Kiel Canal, a major waterway between the Baltic Sea and the North Sea that bisected the Danish peninsula. For this raid we were able to put up forty-two bombers—two air groups of eighteen each with spares. I led one and Nuttall led the other. Another formation of eighteen from the 379th Bomb Group filled out the combat box of fifty-four. The 41st Wing gave me the honor of leading the combat wing box.

The weather was good and we anticipated a successful mission, but none of these raids was ever completed "as briefed," as we often boasted. Something unforeseen was bound to happen. Usually several somethings.

We were to cross the Danish peninsula, do a 180-degree turn over the Baltic, and bomb the canal on a westerly heading. I suppose Bomber Command thought this maneuver would confuse the Jerries and make them think we were headed for a target deeper into Germany. If so, it didn't fool anyone.

Our flight east across the North Sea was peaceful and I had my nose in paperwork. Even in the air there was paperwork. I had a lap chart of the courses, times, and altitudes; a diagram of all aircraft in my two air groups, with names, numbers, and call signs; schedules for what fighter cover we would enjoy (at that time no fighters had the range to accompany us all the way); charts showing known flak emplacements and their coverage; data on merging and breaking up formations; and information on various radio frequencies. When I looked up I was surprised to see land ahead. Islands. Something wasn't right. I checked my watch. We couldn't be making landfall on Denmark. That wouldn't happen for almost an hour.

I looked ahead for the other wings. There were none. "Tail gunner," I called. "Do you see any wings behind us?"

"No, Sir."

"Navigator. What are those islands ahead?"

"Denmark, Sir. North Frisian Islands."

I checked my watch and lap chart again. Those islands couldn't be the North Frisians off the coast of Denmark. What could they be? "Navigator, we haven't flown long enough to make landfall on those Danish islands. Check your work."

"Yes, Sir."

I studied my chart again. According to the time that had elapsed since we left the English coast, those islands had to be the West or East Frisians off the coast of the Netherlands or Germany. A flash of fear ran through me. Here we were making a landfall on German-occupied Europe with only one combat wing. We might get bounced by half the Luftwaffe. I checked the compass in the pilot's compartment. We were on a heading 25 to 30 degrees to the right of our planned course. I didn't wait for the navigator to respond. I knew he must be in a terribly embarrassing funk. Here he had led a whole combat wing of fifty-four bombers on a false course. He could never live this down. His career as a navigator was over.

"Fly due north," I told the pilot. "Let's get out of here. We should intercept the bomber stream up that way."

In a short time I could see the small specks of the wings heading for Denmark. I didn't expect to see wings of our 1st Air Division. We had lost too much time in this navigational snafu. As the specks grew larger and changed to bombers, I saw that they were B-24s of the 2nd Air Division.

I found a space between two of the B-24 wings and elbowed my fifty-four B-17s into line. The 2nd Division leaders didn't like this one bit, and I was roundly castigated. "You B-17s. Get the hell out of our formation. What d'you think you're doing?"

But I wasn't about to go to war with only a one-wing box, and they were only slightly inconvenienced by our joining their bomber stream.

The Luftwaffe must have known where we were going, for it had assembled hundreds of fighters at the base of the Danish peninsula, and all hell broke loose. Enemy fighters bounced us from every direction and altitude, hitting us with every lethal device known to air warfare: guns, rockets, towed bombs—they even dropped bombs set to explode among us.

I coaxed my pilots into a tighter formation with words such as, "Close it up, Cowboys. This is Cowboy leader. Come on, you can tuck them in better than that. Close it up more. Look tough and formidable. Those poor B-24s just can't fly a close formation at this altitude."

The Jerries left us alone. They concentrated on the B-24s.

Those lumbering giants, scattered all over the sky, were exploding and falling like autumn leaves. They didn't have self-sealing fuel tanks as we did, and an incendiary bullet would cause them to burst into a fireball. It was a sickening carnage. Thanks to the hapless B-24s my wing bombed well and lost only one aircraft.

There was a tragic accident in a trailing group, however, caused by another hung bomb problem. Tech. Sgt. Fred S. Wagner had tried to release the hung bombs and had fallen through the open bomb bay. Crewmen from following ships saw him fall and no one saw his chute open. We guessed it was anoxia. He probably had passed out when his walk-around oxygen bottle ran out of the life-giving vapor.*

After this mission I resolved not to fly with just any navigator and bombardier from a lead crew. I chose the best navigator and bombardier in the group, Capt. Robert C. Chapin and Capt. Richard K. Crown, to be my personal crewmen. From that time onward my lead airplane was never off course, and it bombed with spectacular accuracy.

I also leaned on my staff armament officer, Capt. Nathan H. Mazer, a dynamic and imaginative little guy with infectious enthusiasm. I didn't want any more hung bombs. And I think we had no more after that meeting. Nate Mazer, incidently, became one of my most loyal supporters. I didn't have too many.

Bob Williams tried to have a critique after each mission, when all the leaders would rehash what had happened, and ideas would be put forward on how we might improve our air work. I had been disappointed with the leader of the 379th air group, which had flown in the high position, above, to my left and slightly behind my air group. He hadn't always responded to my calls, and sometimes had wandered too far from the wing box. So I reported this at the critique.

The 379th, commanded by Col. Moe Preston, was without

* But Wagner turned up after the war in a POW camp. He had regained consciousness on the way down and pulled his rip cord.

Top: *20th Bomb Squadron, Langley Field, Virginia, shortly before the United States entered World War II.*

Bottom: *Author Paul Gallico, left, boarding B-18 at Langley Field, Virginia, to take part in submarine patrol, summer 1943. Dale Smith is at right, standing.*

Top: *Consolidated LB-30, the lend-lease version of the B-24 bomber, with gun turret moved from tail to nose.*

Bottom: *The new commander of the 384th Bomb Group, Dale Smith, being greeted by Col. Julius K. Lacey, interim commander, at Grafton Underwood.*

Top: *B-17s of the 384th Bomb Group taxiing for takeoff at Grafton Underwood.*

Bottom: *Aerial photo of Grafton Underwood airfield.*

Top: *In Operations Room, 384th Bomb Group.* Left to right: *deputy commander William E. Buck, Dale Smith, and group operations officer Thomas P. Beckett.*

Left: *Dale Smith fully dressed for mission, with oxygen mask, parachute, and flak suit.*

Top: *V-mail Christmas greetings from Dale Smith to family in Reno, Nevada, 1943.*

Bottom: *Group commander's quarters, Grafton Underwood. Staff car is at left. In front of entrance are Colonel Dale Smith* (center), *flanked by orderly, Corporal Whipple* (left), *and driver, Sergeant Montgomery* (right).

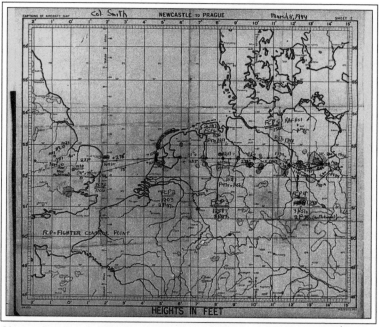

Map used to chart bombing mission against Berlin, March 8, 1944. Notations indicate where P-47 and P-51 fighters arrived to protect against German interceptors. The B-17s of the 384th were over the target at 1429 hours.

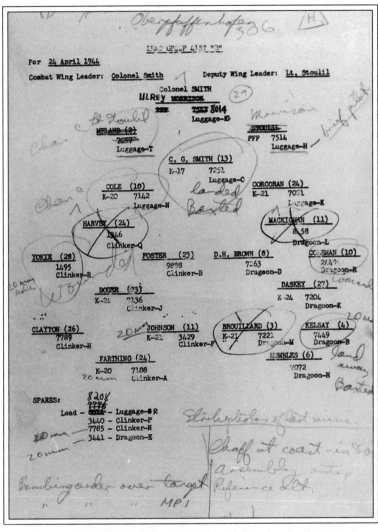

Formation sheet for bombing mission against Oberpfaffenhofen, April 24, 1944. The original aircraft assignments have been penciled over to show missing aircraft, wounded crewmen, and other information. Eighteen B-17s plus two spares flew the mission.

Top: *B-17s in broken cloud cover over enemy country.*

Bottom: *B-17 bomber* Dynamite (in foreground), *as photographed from Dale Smith's B-17 over Berlin, March 8, 1944.*

a doubt the best group in VIII Bomber Command. It had the best record for bombs on the target, for fewest losses and aborts, and almost every other criterion of excellence that was used to measure the groups. I imagine it irked the leader of the 379th air group to have to be subordinate to the 384th, one of the poorer groups, with a commander who was not yet dry behind the ears.

"You led us on a wild goose chase to the Netherlands," he complained. "I wasn't sure what you were going to do."

"You're right about that," I admitted. "That was a stupid goof and I'm sorry. But we recovered, bombed well, and lost only one. So I guess it was a fairly successful mission after all."

Bob Williams broke in. "The combat wing leader is in command. There's no excuse for not following his orders implicitly." And that ended the exchange.

That Kiel mission brought home again the fact that the Luftwaffe fighters tended to pass up the boxes that flew a tight formation and attack those outfits that were loosely stacked or had stragglers. So the way to lower one's loss rate was to fly as if on parade. I had required an experienced pilot to ride in the tail gunner's position on lead airplanes and report any poor formation flying. At group briefings and critiques I asked those pilots who flew sloppily for an explanation. If the explanation involved mechanical trouble I instructed Engineering to go over the affected airplane with a fine-tooth comb. If the poor formation flying was simple pilot error, I'd tell the pilot that he and his crew could not count that mission toward the twenty-five they needed to complete a combat tour. This punishment was felt to be cruel and unusual.

At one of these gatherings, with about five hundred combat crewmen present, the pilot explaining his actions reported that he had "intended" to fly closer but he thought he detected too much prop wash from airplanes ahead of him.

To this I responded with one of my more asinine remarks: "The road to hell is paved with good intentions."

Someone in the back of the room piped up in a loud voice: "So is the road to heaven."

It brought down the house. Everyone enjoyed making me the butt of the joke and I stood there like a wounded bull with nothing to say. If I had had any sense I would have laughed with them, but in those days I took my duties so seriously that nothing much was funny, particularly when it was on me.

On February 14 I led a milk run to Le Meilland, France, to destroy a factory that was turning out war supplies for the German army. But it turned out not to be a milk run after all, and we had to fight our way in and out, losing one bird in the process. This was my seventh mission and I was beginning to get the hang of things. What pleased me most was that fewer and fewer people were treating me like a recruit. Many of the original combat crews were completing twenty-five missions and rotating Stateside. Twenty-five-mission parties were becoming quite common. And the new crews who came to us regarded me as a seasoned veteran.

I flew my eighth mission on February 4, to bomb the docks at Wilhelmshaven again. The weather was bad and we had to use the new H2S radar bombing equipment. It was far better than the old Oboe gear, which depended on radio signals to locate the target, but there was no telling where our bombs landed. We had no losses, although we mourned the fact that Tech. Sgt. Donald I. Collins somehow fell out of his ball turret without a parachute. The ball turret was too small to permit the wearing of a chute.

In February we worked out a system for scheduling group lead officers that helped us plan ahead. Buck, Beckett, and I would take turns, along with the four squadron commanders. Since we were now regularly launching two air groups of eighteen bombers each, that meant that each of us would fly about every third or fourth mission. When we were asked to lead a fifty-four-plane combat wing, however, either Buck or I would usually take the duty. This system relieved much of our anxiety, because we were pretty sure when we would have stand-downs and not have to fly.

Ever since my arrival at Grafton Underwood I had been quartered with Willie Buck and Tom Beckett in a former WAAF (British Women's Auxiliary Air Force) building about four miles from Ops on the other side of the airfield. The road there was twisting and narrow, and the quarters themselves were nothing to boast of. We were required to use blackout headlights on our vehicles, which dimly illuminated only about 10 feet of the road ahead. On cold, dark nights when I was called to Ops to study the frag order, I had to drive at a snail's pace.

I began to scout around the station looking for better and more convenient quarters, and found a permanent building that had once housed a small RAF officers' mess. It was now being utilized by our Quartermaster Company. Trust the Quartermasters to find the best building for themselves! I told the C.O. to find another place for his offices, that I was moving into the building with my staff just as soon as he made it ready for us. He took this with good grace and we soon moved to these very satisfactory digs, which even had a common room where we could have meetings and parties. Now we were in walking distance of the Operations Block and the Officers' Mess, and I was able to get some outdoor exercise on good days.

I also moved my office from the dingy, cold Quonset to the concrete, bomb-proofed Operations Block, which was air-conditioned. I utilized a small cubicle next to the Ops office, with a large window that let me view the many status charts and maps in the Ops Block: a large map of Europe indicating prospective targets and flak emplacements and status boards on lead crews, navigators, bombardiers, aircraft, and so forth. By having these data at my fingertips I could keep better track of what was going on and make better decisions. Willie Buck and Tom Beckett were doubtless not too pleased with my looking over their shoulders this way, but until our record of operations showed considerable improvement I intended to study every aspect of the problem.

Having been a bombardier myself in the early days of service-testing the Norden bombsight, I gave much attention to efforts to improve our poor bombing record. At every opportunity I had the lead crews do practice bombing of a rock in the North Sea. Bad weather hampered this program, however, so I asked Bob Williams if we couldn't send some lead bombardiers to Italy, on TDY with the Fifteenth Air Force, for concentrated bombing practice. Bob cleared this, and for several winter months we rotated lead bombardiers to the good-weather bombing ranges of Italy. By dint of this program and others, our bombing accuracy began to improve.

We took pictures of our bomb strikes and these were sent to the Operational Analysis Group at Bomber Command headquarters. There the strikes were analyzed by professional statisticians and fairly precise records were made of the bombing accuracy. When weather permitted, reconnaissance aircraft would take pictures of the target after our attack to determine what damage had been done. With all this information, along with data on tons of bombs dropped, aborts, and losses, Bomber Command could rank the effectiveness of each bomber group in the Eighth Air Force. I was pleased to see our scores slowly improve. We were no longer at the bottom of the heap.

11

Big Week

The 384th Bomb Group might be improving, but my personal life seemed to be falling apart. The cold, damp English climate got to me and I had two bouts with the flu with temperatures of 103, but our capable flight surgeon soon got me on my feet. What disturbed me more was the lack of news from home, and I visualized all kinds of disasters happening to my family. After January 10 there was no mail from Elise and although I blamed this on the inefficiency of the Army Postal Service, I was uneasy about it.

When I said good-bye to her at La Guardia on that gloomy October day of 1943, I sensed a restraint in her kiss. I knew that she had accused the British of dragging us into their war and she had never approved of my volunteering for duty with the Eighth Air Force when I could just as well have accepted Swede Larson's invitation to go with him to Florida. Now she was being left alone with two small children. Having already lost her only brother she might lose her husband, too.

She was adamant about remaining in New York. The big city fascinated her and she had made many friends. My urging her to move west had only resulted in domestic fights. She didn't want to lose her independence.

For the first few weeks of my absence she wrote long,

passionate letters every day. The trouble was, I hadn't received them. My APO number changed three times in the space of one month and she became confused as to my address, even using an APO number that didn't correspond to any of those I had sent her. Consequently many of her good letters piled up in some Army dead-letter office, and finally came to me in a batch only after Christmas. It was common practice in those days to keep track of correspondence by numbering letters, and by January 3 I noted in my letter number 24 that I was still missing letters from her numbered 3, 4, 6, 7, 8, 9, 15 through 22, and 29. But at least I was beginning to receive letters she had written in December.

The Army Postal Service had developed the V-mail system. If the letter writer used a V-mail form, this would be reduced to 35-mm film, flown across the ocean, printed on paper about the size of a postcard, and delivered by Stateside airmail to the addressee. It was supposed to be faster than regular air mail, and it certainly reduced the amount of air cargo that the Ferry Command had to carry. Transit took about fifteen days.

On January 10 I received a letter from Elise written on Christmas Day. Then for the next month there wasn't a word from her. I was frantic and sent several cablegrams, fearing something terrible had happened to her or the kids. I urged her to respond by cable, but received no answer. I was getting frequent V-mail letters from my parents in Reno. These were beginning to arrive in nine days' time, so I knew the postal service was improving.

On January 31 I was elated to receive a letter from Elise, but it was her number 47 written on December 10. In my number 51 letter to her dated February 6, I wrote: "Still no word since your Xmas day letter, and not even an answer to my cables. I feel so damn helpless. I hope everything is okay with you but I'm terribly worried."

I sent a cable to my friend Frank Matthews at Mitchel

Field, and he was responsible for Elise finally sending me a cablegram. In my letter number 52 dated February 10 I wrote: "My dearest—Yesterday I received your cable and what a relief it was to learn you and the kids are okay. Sorry you have had the flu, and hope the kids don't get it. . . ." But her having the flu didn't explain why she hadn't written for over forty days. I suspected something else was wrong.

On February 15 I wrote:

"My dearest—

Other than your telegram I have not received a single letter from you since #62 written on Xmas day. I can't understand why since I'm getting letters from Reno & sometimes from NYC written in January and February. Please check to see that you are addressing your letters clearly and correctly. Also, at least every 3rd letter send Air Mail, not V-mail. And try using EFM (prepared text) cables. They only cost about 50 cents. I'm sending you one today for Valentine's Day—be mine? Huh? I know it was yesterday but I didn't realize it until someone mentioned it.

Something happened here that I can write to you about [without it being censored]. We had a wedding yesterday! Too bad you couldn't have been here. It all started like this: Some time ago one of our flight leaders Capt. [F. Clinton] Edwards, was wounded & sent to a hospital. There, he fell in love with his American Army Nurse [Dorothea A. Fletcher]. And a couple of weeks ago I granted him permission to get married (big of me, what?) The ceremony was rather Spartan but colorful, nevertheless. It took place in a little cold English church built around 1492 with a reception & wedding cake at the hospital officers' club. It was a beautiful and delicious cake served with—beer. 'S truth, so help me! I shook loose the officers' club here to buy a piece of silver & they found a pretty silver bowl which I presented to the bride as a gift from the group. In addition, I lent them my sedan (the only one on the base) with driver & a rare bottle of scotch to take on their honeymoon to London. I knew that would have been your desire had you been here. You see how well you have trained me!

Of course, almost all of the combat officers from Capt. Edwards' squadron were present, together with the enlisted men from his combat crew. The nurses had us all to supper—poke chops—and wanted us to stay for a Valentine's Party but we found out there was going to be a war on for us the next morning and had to pull out. We all left at 7:30. I must say that there was a good deal of hatred for the Jerries built up over our having to leave.

The officers' clubs I mention are all in Nissen Huts—you know, those kinds of buildings that look like misplaced culverts, with corrigated iron arc sides and tops. But by improvisation they are sometimes fixed up rather nicely.

Well, my dearest, kiss & hug Kort & Voan for me. I wish I could see you all, but someday this will all end. I love you dearly.

Dale

Then on February 19 came a long ambiguous letter from Elise. My answer included this paragraph: "I detect a small voice of ill feeling towards your Old Man in the closing paragraph. You used some expressions you have used in the past when you were good and mad at me. How you can get mad at me now has me whipped—what have I done to hurt you?"

My fears of trouble at home materialized. Elise wrote another long letter on March 14 telling me that Kort had had the flu and Voan was suffering with a serious case of chicken pox.

Moreover, Elise was seeing a doctor about recurring abdominal pains. A week later she wrote from a hospital bed that she had had an emergency appendectomy. Ralph Bucknam's mother, Margaret, who lived in Freeport, Long Island, was taking care of Kort and Voan, with help from Ralph's sister, Alice. Elise's letters were rambling, but without affection.

Elise had not used the medical facilities at Mitchel Field or those of several other local military hospitals. Consequently I was unable to learn anything through the military medical channels as to just how serious were these family health problems. Moreover, the civilian medical expenses were putting us deeper in debt. Letters from friends were optimistic but guarded. Throughout the first three months of 1944 I was troubled and depressed, cut off from all I held dear at home. It was an empty, anchorless feeling.

This was my dark mood as the Eighth Air Force prepared for its biggest bombing offensive to date. The flood of fresh crews and aircraft spurred our high commanders with the desire to flex our new muscle and finally show Germany who was master of the skies over Europe. On February 19 a large high-pressure area was developing over central Germany with the prospect of good bombing weather. That night the teletype brought us orders for a maximum strength mission to attack airfields and aircraft factories deep in central Germany.

A reorganization of the Eighth Air Force had taken place on January 6. Lt. Gen. Ira Eaker, who had built the force from scratch, was sent to command the new Fifteenth Air Force in Italy, and Lt. Gen. James H. Doolittle, of the raid on Tokyo fame, took command of the Eighth. The VIII Bomber Command was disbanded and its headquarters at High Wycombe, a former girl's school north of London, became the new headquarters for the Eighth, while the Eighth's former headquarters at Bushey Park, just south of London, was taken over by Gen. Carl

Spaatz for the new headquarters of the United States Strategic Air Forces in Europe (USSTAF). He would command both the Eighth and the new Fifteenth in Italy.

This reorganization permitted better coordination with escort fighters and the overall operational planning improved. We were beginning to get long-range P-51s and P-47s with drop tanks that would give them the range to escort us deep into Germany. Their success was demonstrated conclusively on the Leipzig mission.

Bomber intruders had always attempted to exploit the chinks in air defense armor. Deceptive maneuvers and feints to throw the enemy defenses off balance were standard practice. Sometimes the bombers were able to attack and withdraw before a tangled German air defense system could reorganize. The broader and deeper the defensive area, the further into the future predictions had to be projected, multiplying the chances for error. Even though we flew into the heart of Germany, defending Luftwaffe fighters sometimes had to fly farther to make contact with the bombers, and the bombers had that much more time to practice deception.

The bombers, of course, generally attempted to pierce the weakest link in the defensive radar chain, and the intruders were sometimes not detected until it was too late for interception. Gaps in early warning radar nets for bombers to sneak through were found with "ferret" aircraft.

Our attacks on enemy fighter plants and airfields near Leipzig on February 20, 1944, presented a striking illustration of bomber deception. German controllers saw our first force, a diversion of three hundred bound for Poland, swing across the North Sea toward Denmark. Believing this a threat to Berlin, the Luftwaffe not only kept their northern fighters in place but dispatched seventy fighters from southern displacements to intercept. Eighty minutes later our main force of seven hundred bombers thrust at Holland on a direct route to the targets. I led the 41st Combat Wing of almost sixty Forts in this bomber stream. German radar stations soon reported our huge strength and before the seventy enemy fighters sent north could intercept our diversionary force their controllers recalled them.

Some ninety local defenders attacked our main force on the penetration to Leipzig, but they had to break off and refuel about target time. The seventy fighters recalled from the north hardly got in the fight before running out of fuel.

Expecting a reciprocal withdrawal, German controllers marshaled all the refueled fighters, together with many others, along our penetration route, ready to swarm upon us on our way out. But we didn't return that way. Instead we turned southwest, detouring in a wide arc south of the Ruhr. By the time German defense commanders discovered our purpose and hastily ordered their assembled fighters south we were well on our way. Only an insignificant number caught the tail of our bomber column as it withdrew to the Channel.

On this occasion it was technically feasible for the enemy air defenses to attack us with a thousand fighters. Warning was perfect, and the fighters were within range. Yet little more than a hundred enemy fighters made contact, in sporadic attacks. This was the result of superior offensive planning by officers on the Eighth's planning staff, who knew how to play football and spoof the opposition again and again.

For once everything seemed to be working right. The 384th had put up two groups for a total of forty-one bombers, and all got off on time. It was a mark of our improved morale that the spares we launched to fill in for possible aborts chose to go to war with us even though there were no aborts. I led one of the air groups from the 384th, and the very capable 1st Lt. Edgar E. Ulrey led the other group, which flew to my left and above me. The 303rd Bomb Group provided the third group box, which was stationed on my lower right, completing the wing combat box.

This was my ninth mission and I was beginning to learn some tricks of the trade. Thanks to the work of our clever and dedicated Intelligence officer, Lt. Col. William E. "Pop" Dolan, and his staff, I had an up-to-date flak chart showing the range of all enemy antiaircraft gun emplacements. Pop didn't trust the flak charts sent to us from Division; they were too often out of date—the Jerries moved their batteries around frequently. Immediately after each one of our missions, at the debriefings, Pop would have his staff carefully question all crew members as to just where the flak they saw was coming from. In this way he updated the Division flak charts. So with the help of his charts I was usually able to weave my way through the barrage of flak we would always encounter on penetrating the enemy coast.

There was one gambit to avoid heavy flak that often worked: when the rounds began to explode near us I'd turn the wing toward the bursts because I knew the flak batteries were tracking us along our course and would be more accurate in the next twenty seconds that it took for a round of flak to reach our altitude. Moreover, the gunners would not be likely to aim again where they had missed. When I saw a cluster of the little black men appear where we might have been if we had continued on the same heading, I knew the trick was working. It was one of the few evasions a great fifty-four plane combat wing could exercise; the huge formation was simply too unwieldy to try any violent evasive maneuvers. It didn't take much for an erratic lead to break up the formation, losing its integrity and mutually supporting firepower.

Another gambit was to keep an eye on the wings ahead to get an idea where the heaviest flak was originating, and then to change course slightly to avoid such a fusillade when we drew near. These tricks worked well for us on the long flight to Leipzig, and although we took some holes, none were serious enough to bring down a Fort or cause an abort.

I was also getting used to the annoying "mad fiddler." This

was high-pitched noise that the enemy broadcast in an attempt to jam our communications. Their tactic never worked very well, for I could almost always hear the transmissions I needed through the dirge of the fiddler. Most of my calls were to leaders in our own wing formation, and we were near enough to each other to receive loud signals. Communications with our fighter escorts were not always as successful, however, either because of the distances involved or because their leaders were too busy fighting to answer.

My communication officers had achieved another innovation that proved to be a great boon to our formation assemblies, as well as to communications on missions. On some operations, when there were decks of clouds in our assembly areas and plans had to be changed, the leader's calls weren't being heard because pilots had switched to interphone and were talking to their crews. So we in the 384th developed the "split headset." One earphone would always be on interphone, and the other always on the command radio. Never would a pilot or copilot be out of touch with either his crew or the formation leaders. External and internal communications were assured at all times.

My group bombed an FW-190 production plant in Leipzig with excellent results. The navigator/bombardier team of Chapin and Crown were in rare form. And Ulrey's group smashed a Luftwaffe airfield to smithereens. We had never bombed as well.

On withdrawal I noticed many contrails far to the south going our way. The distance was too great to see aircraft, but not their telltale contrails. No doubt these contrails were being made by enemy fighters launched late from southern Germany. I asked the tail gunner if we were generating contrails. "Affirmative," he reported, "heavy ones." Sometimes a combat wing would make so many contrails that it appeared to be a long cirrus cloud.

Oh, oh, I thought. If I could see that Luftwaffe leader's

contrails, he could see mine. Yet in the late afternoon we were somewhat up sun from him, and I hoped he hadn't yet spotted us. So I immediately took the wing down into warmer air where we produced no contrails. It worked. The enemy fighters never intercepted.

After we arrived safely at Grafton we were complimented by Generals Travis, Williams, and Doolittle. The mission brought me a Distinguished Flying Cross, which was better deserved by all those 384th troops who had performed so well to make the mission a stunning success. Some weeks later the 384th was honored with a Presidential Unit Citation.

Of the thousand bombers that penetrated to the heart of Germany, we lost only twenty. Friendly fighters had escorted us all the way and had engaged the confused enemy forces. The 384th had no losses.

The Eighth was able to continue this mighty air offensive for the next six days and to thoroughly humble the German Air Force. This Big Week not only curtailed enemy fighter production and damaged many Luftwaffe airfields, but it established the fact that we could penetrate to the heart of Germany day after day and control the air.

POINTBLANK was the code name for the air campaign against the Luftwaffe, its airfields, and supporting facilities. In the end, however, we paid a dear price for Big Week. In all the raids that week American and British losses came to a grand total of four hundred bombers. February 22 in particular was a tragic day for the 384th. We sent seventeen of our triangle "P" bombers to Oschersleben and lost five of them. But we were never stopped or turned back. POINTBLANK was succeeding.

I sometimes wondered how the German populace must have felt to hear the thunderous drumming of the thousands of engines as we cruised into the heart of *der Reich*. At night Bomber Command of the Royal Air Force would rend the air with their engines and bomb cities unmercifully, and in the daytime we would be back with our din from above.

When we were flying there was so much noise from our own engines that we didn't hear the thunder generated by all our cohorts. In fact, we seldom heard the explosions of flak unless they were close. Then we'd get a "whomp," a bump, and sometimes a rattle of shell fragments on our aluminum skin. Enemy bullets fired from fighters would come at us silently, although the response of our own .50s rattled noisily and shook the B-17.

On those days when I was personally stood down I was awed at the rolling thunder overhead as the combat boxes were jockeying for position. The throbbing roar of those thousands of engines seemed to penetrate to my innermost organs, and I wondered how the enemy must have felt as that distant rumble grew louder and louder into a shocking crescendo that signaled a devilish rain of high explosive bombs.

The operational successes of Big Week did little to assuage my black mood. I was extravagantly proud of my group for shaping up so well, and I immersed myself in work, but the demons were let loose at night. I had a vivid nightmare of landing at Leipzig and finding there my little four-year-old, blond daughter covered with bleeding sores. I knew I had to get away from the war for a few days, and I asked Bob Williams to send me to a "Flak House." These were large English estates run by the American Red Cross as havens of rest and recuperation for tired combat crews. Some of my crews had visited one and they gave it high marks.

Living was easy at the Flak House, with clean sheets in soft beds, and charming but entirely proper Red Cross girls as managers and hostesses. I soon got tired of playing parlor games and the food wasn't up to Grafton Underwood's high standards. Bored, I left early and went to London to spend the remainder of my week's leave with brother Thor and Jack Redding at Portsea Hall.

Thor and Jack, who were both lieutenant colonels on General Eisenhower's staff, were busy planning certain features of Operation Overlord, the invasion of the Continent. Out of curiosity I pestered them to tell me when D day would take place. Of course this was one of the deepest secrets of the war and I had no "need to know." They refused adamantly to tell me. Perversely I'd attempt to trick them with questions such as "Will it be in May? June? July?" and study the expressions on their faces. But I never got a clue.

It was verboten for those on combat operations to know such secrets. There was the fear that if one with such knowledge were shot down and questioned by the Germans, the secret might be revealed.

Those few days with Thor and Jack were a catharsis. We argued about the war, but it wasn't the shooting war I was personally involved in, with its repeated heartrending casualties. Instead we argued about the Big Picture, which wasn't particularly traumatic to me. And we drank much scotch and examined all facets of the human equation. They did tell me about the buzz bombs and their "ski sites" being readied in the Pas de Calais for attacks on London. I told them not to worry, boasting that the Eighth would blow the sites sky-high before they ever became operational. They wanted to come to Grafton and fly a mission with me but I refused. There was no need for them to risk their necks just to see the sights. However, I agreed to take them on a practice mission sometime. They were toying with the idea of writing a novel about the Eighth Air Force.

If the Flak House hadn't cured my blues, these stimulating days at Portsea Hall helped me get back on my feet, and I returned to Grafton somewhat refreshed.

12

Berlin

On the last day of February the dangers of V-1, or buzz bomb, attacks on London were beginning to concern the high command, as Thor and Jack had predicted. Captain Edwards led an attack of twenty-four triangle "P" 384th bombers to blow up one of the ski sites. We called them ski sites because the launching devices as seen in the reconnaissance photos looked like skis. Officially they were called Noball targets, whatever that meant.

Although it was a short flight to the Pas de Calais, the mission hadn't turned out to be the milk run we had anticipated. The sites were heavily defended by flak batteries and we lost one of our birds. Moreover, the sites were well camouflaged, hard to hit, and easy to repair. My remark that we would blow them up before they became operational was an empty boast. It wasn't long before the frightening flying bombs were falling at random on London.

During the first week in March I received a call from Bill Gross, my classmate who commanded the 1st Combat Wing. His headquarters was at Bassingbourn, a former permanent RAF station of imposing brick buildings. It was the only permanent base in the Eighth Air Force, and when VIPs came to England to see how the war was being fought, Generals Spaatz and Doolittle always took them to Bassingbourn. There was a famous group stationed there, too, the 91st. It had led the first Bomber Command raid on Schweinfurt, August 17, 1943, when the Luftwaffe had nearly destroyed our daylight bombing effort. Col. Bill Gross had led that killer mission, although Gen. Bob Williams had gone along in another B-17 as the nominal commander of the raid.

Bill wanted me to come to Bassingbourn and help him entertain a group of VIPs headed by the new Secretary of State E. R. Stettinius, Jr. Generals Spaatz and Doolittle would be there and a host of other bigwigs. I agreed and drove the forty miles in time for cocktails at the Officers' Club. Bill had me seated between the secretary and General Spaatz. Mostly I listened and answered a few questions.

The dour Gen. "Tooey" Spaatz held forth on his ideas of fighter cover. He believed they shouldn't stick so close to the bombers in a defensive posture, but should sweep far and wide to attack Luftwaffe formations and airfields wherever they were found. This tactic, he believed, would more quickly subdue the German Air Force. I never felt we had a plethora of fighter escorts, and wasn't too enthusiastic about General Spaatz's proposed strategy. I made a rebuttal, which wasn't given much consideration. Before many weeks had passed I saw fewer and fewer fighter escorts. Although their numbers increased, they were off looking for enemy Jagstaffels and building up their score of kills.

The handsome and lively secretary of state had much to say about politics, which I knew nothing about. One remark of his, however, rang a loud alarm in my head. He said casually: "We're expecting a lot from you men during the next three months."

The next three months! We'd been fighting the war for two years so what was significant about the next three months? It took no mathematical genius to figure the next three months put us to the first week in June. Of course. D day! He had inadvertently revealed almost to the very day the super-secret date of the planned Allied invasion of the Continent.

Secretary Stettinius had no idea that I wasn't privy to that highly classified information, but in any event he shouldn't have made such a thoughtless remark. If it were known that I knew when D day was, I'd be taken off combat operations. The invasion date was so secret that General Eisenhower didn't want to risk the chance that someone shot down on an Eighth Air Force mission might spill the beans. The Jerries had some diabolical means of winnowing the truth from prisoners of war. They were even known to use truth drugs.

I looked at Tooey Spaatz and expected him to take me off Operations on the spot, but he studiously dissected his tough steak and said nothing. Could he have thought I was too stupid to figure out the obvious? Or did he trust that the enemy could never get that vital date out of me? More likely he just hadn't heard the secretary's remark.

I was beginning to understand why the Jerries knew so much about us. Too many people knew too many secrets, and civilians were not trained in keeping their mouths shut. They didn't appreciate the dire consequences of loose talk. If Hitler knew the time and place of the invasion it would cost thousands of Allied lives and the invasion might be thwarted. We could even lose the war.

Perhaps I should have taken myself off Operations, but with the 384th shaping up so well I couldn't risk it. The men just wouldn't understand if I stood myself down for three months until D day. I wouldn't be able to tell them why. Moreover, I was supremely confident that I could hold my tongue if captured by the enemy. So I let the matter ride. It wouldn't be the first time I had overlooked orders from Bushey Park.

The next time I saw Thor I teased him by claiming that by reading his expression he had revealed to me that D day was June 5. He blew his top, and I had to confess that no other than the secretary of state had leaked this information to me.

After the successes of the Big Week offensive we knew that the next big air operation would be against Berlin, or Big B as we called it. The RAF Bomber Command had been hitting Berlin at night, but Hitler's capital had never been bombed in daylight. Reconnaissance reports revealed that it was the most heavily defended target in Germany, and we dreaded the missions that were sure to come.

Beside my bed I had a Zenith portable radio, and I often listened to propaganda broadcasts from Berlin. It was uncanny how much the Jerries knew about us. They not only knew we were planning to bomb Berlin, but they named the officers who were commanding our groups, and once I even heard my own name mentioned. We'd tune to these enemy stations because the music was more our style than what we got from British radio. The German DJs would taunt us that we'd be slaughtered if we tried to bomb Berlin, and we half believed them. Air Marshal Hermann Göring, leader of the German Air Force, boasted that if American bombers reached Berlin his name would be Meyer. There was no doubt about it, a raid on Berlin would be a bloody battle.

Several times we'd been briefed for Big B, but each time the missions had been scrubbed because of bad weather. However, on the third of March, Eighth Air Force took a chance with marginal weather and launched a raid. It was a mistake, because unusually high clouds were found over the Continent and the whole force had to be recalled.

General Doolittle tried again on the fourth, but the weather was still marginal. Major Raymond P. Ketelsen, the veteran commander of the 545th Squadron, led our triangle Ps but failed to assemble with the wing or the division because the wing leader was flying too fast. A short way into Germany the weather deteriorated to such an extent that the mission was again recalled by Eighth Air Force. Ketelsen's wing leader ordered him to bomb a target of opportunity. Fifteen of our Forts bombed through a solid overcast on the signal of the radar aircraft, or pathfinder (PFF), believing the target to be Bonn although we later learned it was Cologne. It was a very poor show for the

384th. Of the twenty-two we launched there were seven aborts. Three others failed to return.

Twenty-nine B-17s of 3rd Division didn't hear the recall signal and proceeded to Berlin over the high cloud bank. They bombed through the overcast and lost five in the ensuing fierce battle. These Forts, from the 95th and 100th groups, were the first American heavies to strike Berlin.

Berlin was becoming a jinx target for the Eighth, and even more so for our group. In his routine report to me on the mission Pop Dolan had this to say about our seven aborts:

1.b. A/C 112 (Capt. Thompson, pilot) turned back at 1048 hours . . . because #1, #2 and #3 engines were smoking very badly after pulling excessive manifold pressure for approximately thirty minutes.

A/C 801 (Lt. H. C. Smith, pilot) turned back at 0955 hours . . . because of oxygen failure. Dropped from 350 lbs. to 250 lbs. in thirty minutes without use.

A/C 495 (Lt. Foster, pilot) turned back to 1018 hours . . . because #2 and #3 engines were running rough and smoking.

A/C 792 (Lt. Pryer, pilot) turned back at 1018 hours . . . because engineer was knocked out while fixing the ball turret. . . .

A/C 014 (Lt. Jorgenson, pilot) turned back at 1010 hours . . . because fuel transfer pump was inoperative.

A/C 364 (Lt. West, pilot) turned back at 1035 hours . . . because it took off late and was unable to locate group formation due to poor visibility.

A/C 449 (Lt. Daskey, pilot) turned back at 1007 hours . . . torn off.

Needless to say I was mightily displeased by this disgraceful performance, but I tended to blame much of it on the poor wing leadership of another group. No effort had been made to slow or zigzag that lead group so that trailing groups could join, and Ketelsen's group, in their attempt to catch up, exceeded the capabilities of many B-17 Wright Cyclone engines.

We stood down on the next day, March 5. But a maximum effort was ordered for the sixth. Again the target was Big B. We launched twenty-four Forts. Six of them, under command of Lt. Earl T. Allison, were to join a composite group. The remaining eighteen were led by Maj. Carl L. Lyles, who had been sent to us by the 41st Wing. For what I considered unjustified reasons he aborted the whole group, explaining that he had had assembly trouble.

Not only was I mortified by this abysmal showing, but so were most of the people in the group. Only a few came to the line to watch the landing once word got out what had occurred. Everyone was embarrassed and crestfallen. I wondered if the 384th was again in the slump I had found it in when I joined last November. I believed our esprit de corps had been steadily growing. Certainly up to now our air work had improved along with conditions on the ground. Had I been fooling myself with wishful thinking?

There was one bright spot. Five of Allison's squadron had gone to Berlin with the composite wing and had bombed with PFF through low clouds. They reported moderate flak and excellent fighter support from P-51s, P-47s, and P-38s. There were no losses, but they had one abort.

One of Allison's planes was piloted by George B. West, who had aborted two days before because he took off late and couldn't find the group formation. But on this mission to Berlin he and his brave crew flew to the target and back with minimum life-giving oxygen. Hundreds of miles from Berlin on the way in, a defective valve had caused the loss of a fourth of their supply. "How many of you men want to keep right on to Berlin?" he asked his crew over the interphone, and then kept talking without waiting for a reply: "Well, you're going!" West sent his engineer, Tech. Sgt. Creig B. Crippen, back to the ball turret where the leak had occurred and he patched the oxygen lines. By dint of much innovation and clever oxygen management Lieutenant West completed the mission. He should have been decorated for this gutsy performance, which was an example to everyone in the group, but no one was thinking about decorations that day.

The jinx still hounded the Eighth Air Force. Other groups hadn't fared as well as the group Allison was with. Over seven hundred heavy bombers had been dispatched, supported by nearly eight hundred escort fighters. The bomber stream was sixty miles long, and under vicious attack by the Luftwaffe for most of the way. Our escorts couldn't cover all the wings and the Jerries bounced those that were least protected. Bombs were aimed by PFF, and none of the primary targets were hit. Losses amounted to 69 heavies, while 3 that returned had to be scrapped and 102 had major battle damage. It was the bloodiest day the Eighth had suffered.

I imagined everyone in the Eighth Air Force would regard the 384th as quitters when the going got tough. Both Generals Travis and Williams conveyed their displeasure in no uncertain terms. Moreover, I criticized myself for not having led the group. I could have objected to the wing's selection.

As a rule, group commanders only led when their groups were leading combat wings. That is, when the 384th was ordered to lead the 41st Combat Wing composed of the 384th, 303rd, and 379th, then the 384th commander was usually designated the wing leader. I had followed this custom, but there was no rule that said a group commander couldn't fly whenever he chose to, and considering the importance of the target, I knew now that I should have flown on the sixth.

An abort because of weather was usually justified. Flying different positions in the sky, each formation leader saw different banks of clouds and had to make his own decision. It wasn't very healthy to lead large formations of B-17s through heavy clouds. It was like taxis trying to operate in a pea-soup London fog except that when a collision occurred in the air that was all, brother.

Our group abort on the sixth was another matter. The leader had simply failed, through poor navigation and worse pilotage, to join the wing formation. Instead of joining another wing and going to war, he elected to return home.

I hoped we could all get to Big B on the next effort and prove to the Eighth, the 1st Air Division, and the 41st Combat Wing that the 384th was a worthy outfit. I didn't have long to wait.

On the night of March 7, my birthday, a frag order came over the teletype directing us to lead the wing to Big B. That meant me, although I had decided to lead the group in any event.

That night I dreamed that two German commandos armed with submachine guns entered my room and snatched the yellow frag order from my bedside table. As the men withdrew I yelled and reached for the loaded pistol hanging in its shoulder holster just behind my head. When I saw the frag order was still on the table I realized it was only a dream.

Following the general briefing I asked all pilots to stand by and I urged them to stay with the formation and not abort, making the boast that I was going to Berlin if I had to fly there alone. One or two spoke up: "We'll go with you, Colonel!" Then all of them broke in with similar assurances. I'm afraid my talk reflected an unjustified disappointment with the group. After all, they weren't to blame for our disgrace of the sixth.

Our target was the ball bearing factory at Erkner, just east of Berlin, where since the Schweinfurt raids most of Germany's ball bearings were now being manufactured. Weather had finally cleared. It was a perfect day over Germany. We penetrated Holland north of Amsterdam and proceeded toward the Zuider

Zee. Our combat wing of fifty-four was the fifth in the stream and I could see the four ahead of us like swarms of bees, diminishing to mere specks in the distance. This gave me a particular advantage. I could watch the flak bursts aimed at the wings ahead and get a fair idea of where the batteries were located. I guided our wing away from those dangers. We were getting a free ride.

This worked pretty well up until we crossed the Zuider Zee. I had selected a path that had been free of flak. But perhaps a battery was just coming into action, because suddenly great bursts appeared right in the midst of our formation. I had never seen such accurate enemy fire on the first salvo. It was phenomenal. Unfair! Before I could even think of taking evasive action with the formation, a shell went through my left wing and exploded a few feet above, rocking our ship and sprinkling it with metal fragments. I stared in chilled alarm at the gaping hole, as wide as the cover of a GI can with aluminum skin curling up around the edges.

Certainly the wing tanks were punctured and I tensed for the inevitable explosion. But nothing happened. How could we still be flying? Both left engines purred undisturbed. But surely the aileron cables would be sheared. Carefully I tested the controls. The wings dipped normally. A miracle! It didn't make sense, but I thanked God and breathed a sigh of relief. We wouldn't have to abort or bail out. We could go on. I could live up to my boast.

When we reached the outskirts of Berlin, flak and fighters struck us with fiendish force. But our "Little Friends" in their P-51s and P-38s were there as well, and the Luftwaffe had no field day. A few minutes after arriving at the Initial Point where the groups separated from the wing formation in preparation for bombing, our Fort bucked as if hitting something.

"What was that?" I called to Chapin in the greenhouse.

"A P-38 diving on an ME-109 just missed us," he replied.

The air was getting as crowded as a gridlocked highway but I was comforted by this close protection.

Our target at Erkner was partially covered with a German smoke screen, so Crown used offset sighting and managed to get a good pattern on the ball bearing plant. Then it was dive and turn to throw off the flak, reform the combat wing box, and head for home. Once through the gauntlet of flak around Berlin it was pretty smooth sailing. I gave that accurate flak battery in Holland a wide berth.

But our troubles weren't over. The clear weather we had enjoyed when leaving England had worsened. On crossing the Channel we found a solid undercast over the whole of the British Isles. On checking with our base we learned that it was socked in with thick fog and that there were no open alternates within range of our dwindling fuel supply. We'd been practicing instrument letdown procedures but they weren't honed to handle such low ceilings. If I attempted to get into Grafton I might prang several Forts on the hills and obstructions.

I had anticipated such a nightmare situation and knew what I was going to do. By now I had relieved the other two groups from the combat wing box and the 384th was on its own. We had nineteen in the formation now, for which I was responsible. Not far from Grafton was the great bay on the North Sea called The Wash. I headed there and searched for a hole in the clouds below us. There wasn't much time. Our fuel was low.

Luck was with us. A small hole appeared through which I spotted some whitecaps. I put the formation in a wide echelon to the right and told the pilots to follow me through the hole. Then I dove, pulling out just above the rough water. Soon the 384th was again in echelon below the clouds, skimming the water and heading for England.

We made landfall and hedgehopped through the scud, just missing church steeples and power lines. It must have shocked the people of the villages we passed. Nineteen Flying Fortresses with seventy-six engines just overhead made a frightful thunder.

The ceiling began to lift some and I sent the formation on to Grafton Underwood, while I landed at a nearby RAF field. I wanted to check that hole in my wing.

Big B was behind us. It was a successful mission. We had had three aborts but two spares had joined the group and we had bombed Erkner with nineteen and had no losses. From all reports Captain Crown, our lead bombardier, had put our bombs squarely on the target. We would never fear Big B again. The 384th could fly anywhere in Germany, hit its target, and prevail. We could hold up our heads again and be beholden to no other group in the Eighth.

I was hoisting a warm scotch with my hospitable Royal Air Force hosts when my engineer reported on the condition of our ship.

"Colonel," he said, "that flak that went through your wing?"

I nodded.

"Well, it sheared the main spar. I don't see how the wing stayed on. You'll never be able to fly that B-17 again."

Only the skin on the wing had held it together into and out of Berlin! How in the world could it have withstood that dive and sharp pullout through the hole in the clouds? I took a big gulp of RAF scotch and said a silent prayer of thanks to all the builders of that rugged, tough old warhorse, and to the angel who was looking over my shoulder.

It was a long hard drive home that night, in a British "lorry" so small I couldn't get comfortable enough to sleep. It was driven by a serious little British WAAF. I don't know how she found her way in the rain and fog, but we arrived before dawn and had a delicious breakfast with the combat crews who were preparing to attack Oranienburg, Germany. This was another target near Berlin. Willie Buck, Tom Beckett, and Pop Dolan would brief them, and Al Nuttall would lead the mission. Their spirits were high and I was confident everything would turn out right.

All our birds had landed safely the night before. My only concern now was to hit the sack for a week or two. I was bone tired, but deliriously happy that the triangle Ps had performed so well with no losses.

That day Al Nuttall led a good raid on an Oranienburg aircraft factory and returned with no losses. We flew ten more missions in March of 1944 with the loss of only four aircraft and very few aborts. The 384th was on a roll.

13

Marienburg

Thor and Jack Redding came to Grafton Underwood in late March to get material for their book, *Wake of Glory*. Again they pestered me to let them go on a combat mission, but I was just as determined as before not to approve it. However, I did live up to my promise to take them on a practice mission. I scheduled these as frequently as possible in order to drill the pilots in close formation flying and give the bombardiers and navigators some hands-on training. We'd zigzag over East Anglia as we did when forming wings on combat missions, then fly up to The Wash and bomb Scares Rock.

I had decided to fix up one of the recently acquired silvershiny B-17Gs as my personal airplane and had the sub-depot put armor plate beneath the pilot and copilot seats. I had been sitting on my flak vest up to now, but with this armor plate that protected my most valuable parts I could now wear the vest. I hadn't given the new bird a name yet, and I asked Thor and Jack to help me select one.

They flew with me in this new bird on the practice mission. I didn't put myself in the lead, but flew separately so that I could observe the formation from several angles as well as judge the skills of the squadron and group leaders.

On the way to and from Scares Rock I'd call to pilots who were a little out of formation and tell them to close up. Those who were far out of line I'd order to leave the formation and watch where I flew. (Formation flying had been one of my favorite sports in flying school.) Then I'd slide my silver bird into the slot left by the vacated B-17. Pulling up as close as I dared to the leader, I'd call to the pilot of the B-17 that I'd pulled out of the formation, "See, this is how I want you to fly. Get in real tight."

Shaming pilots who flew poor formation wasn't the best kind of leadership, and perhaps I was showing off to Thor and Jack. Nevertheless our formation flying was improving, and with it we were losing fewer airplanes on missions. A pilot in the practice formation had his radio on when he thought he was speaking on interphone. Or maybe he knew he was on radio; in any event, he broadcast, for all in the formation to hear, "Listen to that goddamn screaming eagle. I wish he'd shut up." He was referring, of course, to the colonel's eagles and the guy wearing them.

Thor and Jack heard this, and after landing Thor said, "I've got the name for your airplane."

"Oh? What is it?"

"Why don't you call it 'Screaming Eagle'?"

We all laughed. "That's it," I said as I turned to the ship. "I hereby christen you *Screaming Eagle.*"

The nose artists did a nice job of giving number 007 a new name and I imagine many a combat crewman, sick and tired of hearing me harangue them, got a chuckle out of it.

Sometime later I received a telephone call from Bassingbourn. It was Bill Gross. "I got my star!" he yelled into the phone. "Let's celebrate!"

"Congratulations, Maestro! It's about time." Bill had been holding down a general's job as combat wing commander for several months, but his promotion had been slow in coming. Perhaps it was because he was such a junior colonel. At last the West Point class of 1934 had a brigadier general. He was the first.

"Can you meet me tonight in London, at Thor's?" Bill

always made up his agile mind in a hurry. Nothing was impossible for him.

"I don't see why not. I'm overdue for a forty-eight-hour pass."

"Joe Nazarro will be with us. You know him, don't you? The commander of my 381st group?"

I told him I knew Joe well. When I was at Polebrook Joe had invited me to visit his base. I'm afraid I had kept Joe up most of the night as we boiled his precious eggs in a mess tin over a coke stove, while I quizzed him about the task of leading B-17s in the war. He had helped me a lot.

"Okay, then it's on," Bill concluded. "Some friends of Joe's in London want us to come see them. But we'll find plenty else to do."

"Yes, Sir, *General*," I responded.

"Oh, knock it off! I'll see you tonight."

My conscientious orderly, Sgt. Bob Montgomery, drove me the eighty miles to London while I slept in the back seat of our beat-up Plymouth. He dropped me at Portsea Hall and then went on to the Red Cross Club to spend the night. Bill was already at Thor's and they were making a big dent in Bassingbourn scotch. Joe Nazarro soon joined us and we began making the rounds of London night clubs.

Joe had been an all-round athlete at West Point as well as probably the best-looking cadet in his class. With a dazzling smile and winning personality, people flocked to him. With Joe, we made friends wherever we went.

Thor took us to his "club" somewhere in a basement that had survived the blitz. There, by candlelight, we enjoyed a delicious steak. "How come they can get steak?" I asked Thor, and he shrugged. I took out my Zippo lighter and studied the menu. There, in very fine print at the bottom of the page, I found: "Horsemeat sold here." That answered my question, and although I could find no fault with the steak I never joined Thor's "club."

Joe Nazarro and I "sirred" and saluted Bill at every opportunity. We'd snap to attention whenever he spoke and showed him all kinds of exaggerated deference. Bill got so angry that he was ready to fight us both. We finally had to stop hazing him about his new stars, for fear we'd all get in trouble.

Next day we dressed in our best uniforms and took a taxi out to a suburb to visit Joe's friends. After dismissing the taxi we stopped dead still, listening to the distant rumble of a buzz bomb. Its unmistakable engine noise sounded much like a motorcycle and the frightening rumble grew louder and louder. Bill pointed. "There it is!" It was coming right for us. We stared in fascination. If its engine kept going it would fly over us and spin in beyond us to explode in some other neighborhood.

The winged bomb grew larger and larger until it was directly overhead. Then its engine stopped. We didn't wait to see it heel over and start for the ground. The three of us dived under a parked truck and held our breath.

WHAM! The explosion rocked our bodies and hammered on our ears. The bomb had landed three blocks away, blowing up four houses.

We pulled ourselves from under the truck and examined our oil-stained uniforms. What a mess. Then we realized that the people who were in those crushed houses might need some help, and we ran to the smoking ruins. There wasn't much we could do. We saw no bodies, and in minutes the fire engines were there with rescue teams.

Sometime later Gen. Dwight D. Eisenhower visited Bassingbourn. He wanted to meet all the Eighth Air Force group commanders. So we assembled in Bassingbourn's Officers' Club and were each introduced to the man who commanded the greatest invasion in history. He gave us a short pep talk while we stood around with weak drinks in our hands. I imagine he was hoping we'd clear the skies over Normandy.

At Grafton I was still working on the idea of integrating my ground and air personnel in order to improve our teamwork and mutual respect. It occurred to me that if the ground officers flew one mission they would better understand what the combat crews were up against; also, it would give the ground pounders a bit more pride. After all, they were soldiers, too, and in a combat theater. With one mission under their belts they could truthfully tell their wives and sweethearts that they had been at war. In addition, the air personnel on the base would pay them more respect. Hence I directed Willie Buck and Jim Taff to encourage ground officers to fly at least one mission, and to schedule those who volunteered. Tom Beckett was to send them on milk runs such as Noball bombings in the Pas de Calais.

The trouble was that there were no milk runs. Not long after this policy went into effect, a well-liked ground officer, the base administrative inspector, Maj. Russell H. Sanders, was killed by a direct flak hit to his plane. Those in the group who considered my policy unnecessary and heartless were highly critical. My stock dropped; some few regarded me as no less than a murderer. But I weathered the storm, and ground officers continued to fly. Some, such as Pop Dolan and Nate Mazer, flew several missions. Nate even won an Air Medal. I believe this practice did much to improve the overall esprit and effectiveness of the group. Major Sanders did not die in vain.

It's interesting to note that those few who were most critical of the policy never flew on a mission.

When the British were stationed at Grafton Underwood they had used a public address system, with speakers in every building. The 384th had considered this Tanoi communication system an unnecessary invasion of privacy and had never put it into use. To me it seemed like a good way to get word to all the troops, and I ordered it repaired and made operational.

One thing that bothered me was that when combat crews were stood down they tended to stay in the sack most of the day.

We kept training schedules in all aspects of operations, but attendance was spotty. I didn't want to institute a reveille call and formation or have calisthenics before breakfast, as was customary in the old Army, but I did want everyone to get up for breakfast and establish some sort of routine. So I directed that the duty officer in the Operations Block would announce over the Tanoi: "Good morning. It's six-thirty. Let's put the show on the road."

Before my time with the 384th, the well-liked air exec, Lt. Col. Seldon L. McMillen, had gone down on a mission, and after several weeks a postcard arrived from a POW camp in Germany. It was from McMillen and he wrote, "Let's keep the show on the road." This motto caught on like wildfire, and became a part of the group insignia. So no complaints ever got to me about the Tanoi wake-up calls.

The Tanoi had many other valuable uses. After each mission the duty officer would announce the results: number of planes off, number of aborts, number missing, what the target was, how accurate the bombing was, and any other pertinent information. Thus every man on the base knew just how well the group had done as soon as possible after the Forts returned. This information might have been helpful to the Jerries, but I believed it was more important that all 384th personnel should feel intimately involved with our mission.

Later on I had each squadron fly formation over the field on return from a mission. A committee of lead pilots from each squadron would judge the best formation and that night over the Tanoi I'd announce which squadron won the contest. There was some grumbling about this; the crews were understandably tired and anxious to get on the ground. But I argued that champions always sprinted the last hundred yards, no matter how tired they were. This competition did much to improve our formation flying.

I also used the Tanoi to announce the imminent advent of

visiting VIPs. When General Travis was due to inspect us I warned, "Anyone not saluting General Travis will be hanged by his thumbs from the control tower." Later the general remarked on the snappy salutes he had received from all personnel.

On April 8, 1944, General Travis invited me to dinner at his 41st Combat Bomb Wing headquarters. It was a gala affair, with his other group commanders present along with his senior staff and a number of RAF group captains.

Bob Travis never wanted to be second best at anything. He was the best skeet shot, owner of the best over-and-under double-barreled gun I ever saw, the best poker player (I had unhappily contributed to this aspect of his reputation when we had both served at Luke Field, Hawaii, before the war), the best chess player (next to crapshooting and chasing women it had become the most popular indoor game of the Eighth Air Force middle-level brass), the best-dressed (his uniforms, made of the most expensive material, were tailored to perfection), and he was well on the way to becoming one of the most highly decorated generals of the Army Air Forces. His dinner party was graced with some of the most attractive, well-coiffed, and well-gowned women I had ever seen in England, but I never got the chance to get acquainted with any of them.

After my first bite of steak, which proved to be the best I had ever tasted on that side of the Atlantic, I knew something was up. An aide whispered in Bob's ear, and Bob passed a message to his Operations officer. Bob rose and motioned me to a quiet corner where he whispered: "A field order just came in for tomorrow. It's a big one. Marienburg in East Prussia. Your group's leading the wing on this one."

I nodded, and as usual my stomach contracted as I realized I would soon be flying over Germany.

"Who do you recommend as wing leader?" he asked.

"It's my turn," I responded, my heart heavy in my chest.

Although I'd participated in twelve missions, each one presented a dreadful terminal prospect, and I couldn't take it impersonally.

"Okay," Bob said. "You'd better get going. Good luck."

Departing without further discussion, I drove the fifteen or so miles from Kimbolton to Grafton Underwood. There I went directly to my office in the Operations blockhouse, that austere reinforced concrete structure half underground.

Willie Buck and Tom Beckett brought me the frag order along with a stack of other data. The Ops staff and Pop Dolan's Intelligence staff had already made the schedules and plans down to the last detail. Nothing was left for me to do but comment on certain points and commend them for their rapid, thorough, and meticulous work. As always, a major worry was the weather. The forecast for England didn't look good, although the route and target would probably be clear.

I crawled into the sack at 1:15 A.M., only to be awakened at 4:30 by the jangle of a wake-up telephone call from Ops. Hastily dressing in the frigid hut, I emptied my pockets and deposited the contents, along with my West Point ring, in the old dresser. Then I drove slowly, with dim blackout lights, to the Officers' Mess.

Inside it was glaring with lights and bustling with combat crews talking excitedly and enjoying the treat of fresh eggs and bacon provided only to those scheduled for a mission. For me, the pleasure was marred by the pit of fear in my stomach, and I wondered how many others were so afflicted. Who among us would be eating his last meal?

Next stop was the large briefing auditorium. The crews were waiting as I strode up the aisle with as much confidence and insouciance as I could muster. All stood to attention, sort of. Leaping onto the low stage, taking care not to trip, I turned and said:

"At ease, gentlemen. Be seated.

"Today our target is a Focke-Wulf 190 assembly plant. If we clobber it there won't be so many enemy fighters after us in the future. So I know you won't miss.

"There's a bonus in this raid. The Eighth hit this same plant last October, and it's taken until now to get it back on line. To celebrate the occasion, Intelligence tells us that Hermann Göring will be there. We'll strike just about the time he's to make his speech. If we don't hit him, we'll at least spoil his whole day.

"But it's no milk run. It's one of the longest missions we've ever had. We'll be at maximum weight and will climb out slowly to conserve fuel. Tanks will be topped off at twenty-seven hundred gallons after engine warm-up. Keep your mixtures lean and your RPMs low. We'll have just enough fuel to get home.

"Now here it is!"

Pop Dolan dramatically pulled the drawstrings, and the curtain parted to reveal a large map of Europe. Red yarn stretched over the North Sea, across the Jutland peninsula, east through the Baltic Sea (where the map had to be extended), then southeast on a dogleg to Marienburg, a few miles from Danzig (now Gdansk) in Poland.

Reacting to the distant target, four hundred or so men lounging in leather flight jackets and fifty-mission caps filled the room with whistles, catcalls, and groans. I stepped down and took my seat by the aisle. There I found the bundle of paperwork I'd need to lead the group and wing—route charts, diagrams of formations with aircraft numbers and pilots noted, call signs and frequencies, flak charts, fighter rendezvous, IPs, etc.

Ops briefed on formations, assembly routes, and rendezvous; Intelligence on flak and expected enemy fighters; Armament on bomb load and ammo. We would each carry twelve 500-pound general purpose bombs. Communications covered frequencies, call signs, and gave us a time hack. Weather gave us the latest guesses: it still looked very bad over England:

layers of broken clouds to 12,000 feet. Target briefing had been held earlier for lead navigators and bombardiers. Pop had flashed the latest reconnaissance pictures of the target and aiming points on a screen and described them in detail. Ballistic winds were estimated to help the bombardiers. Nothing was left to chance.

I gave what I hoped was a short pep talk and asked for questions. There were none. "That's all. Good luck!"

Next stop was the personal equipment room, where we suited up with electrically heated underwear and boots. Over the wired long johns I wore a summer flying suit and the habitual leather jacket. I wrapped a large piece of black-dyed parachute silk around my neck and donned a warm leather helmet with built-in earphones. Next came a Mae West life vest and chest chute harness. I packed an A-3 bag with my detachable barrel chute, flak vest, electrically heated gloves, and a rebreather oxygen mask. An Intelligence officer handed me an escape kit, which fit in the knee pocket of my flying suit and included a silk waterproof map of Europe, German marks, a compass, and other useful items to facilitate evasion. Finally, we were handed our lunch, a Milky Way bar.

My driver, Sgt. Bob Montgomery, had caught up with me and stood by the old staff car as I emerged with my gear. He took my A-3 bag and threw it in the trunk. I invited the group bombardier, Capt. Dick Crown, and the group navigator, Capt. Bob Chapin, to join me. Other crews were being delivered to the dispersed hardstands around the field where the loaded Flying Fortresses crouched. There was a continuous parade of growling, blacked-out five-ton trucks, like one streetcar after another.

On *Screaming Eagle*'s pad I met Capt. Earl T. Allison and his crew, who would man the lead ship of the formation. Recently promoted, Allison had proved himself an outstanding pilot and leader, having been one of the few 384th pilots who refused to

abort in bad weather on the March 6 mission to Berlin. He'd fly
and I'd ride in the copilot's seat, while his own copilot would
take the tail gunner's position and report to me on formation
dispositions and other matters. Thus I would have eyes in the
back of my head. Allison's navigator would assist Chapin in the
nose, but his bombardier would stand down while Crown took
his place.

Our crew chief had been up all night with his ship and had
just shut down the engines and topped off the tanks. He reported the silver B-17 ready to fly. There wasn't much to do but
kick the tires, squeeze through the hatches, get settled with our
gear, and go through our checklists.

Start engines was signaled with a yellow-red flare from the
control tower. We kept scrupulous radio silence. There was no
sense in advertising our mission any sooner than necessary. The
German Würzburg radars would pick us up soon enough. Seconds before the flares popped we had wound up our whining
inertial starters, so that as the flares lit, the first forty big Wright
Cyclone engines coughed into life.

Seconds later the air vibrated with the rumble of 160 idling
engines. A yellow-green flare signaled us to taxi, and the heavy
bombers waddled into line on the taxi strip surrounding the
field, with *Screaming Eagle* taking the lead at the end of the
takeoff runway. It was SOP for us to take off at thirty-second
intervals, and that meant exactly thirty seconds, not twenty-
nine or thirty-one. Successful group assembly depended on this
kind of timing.

Ahead was a low broken overcast, with ominous scud on
the horizon at the end of the runway. I exchanged worried
glances with Earl Allison as we studied the sky. It was going to
be touchy enough getting the overloaded Fort into the air. And
now we'd be on instruments even before our wheels were up.

Our ship trembled as Allison shoved the throttles forward
and revved up the engines to takeoff RPM. Then a green-green

flare stabbed the darkness. Earl released the brakes: more precision. A relentless well-oiled war machine, I thought. But all this comforting order was soon dissipated in chaos and confusion.

Screaming Eagle accelerated sluggishly with its great load, and the end of the runway was almost upon us when she broke ground. I quickly raised the gear to streamline the ship and began monitoring the flight instruments as the low clouds enfolded us.

Our group assembly pattern was simple and well rehearsed. The leader would climb straight ahead for X number of minutes at a prescribed rate of climb and airspeed and then make a broad precision turn to the left, bringing him back on a reciprocal course next to the field. Following aircraft would turn Y number of seconds sooner than the ones ahead, thus bringing us all together in an eighteen-plane group box formation. But this maneuver was predicated on good weather. As I passed the field running in and out of clouds at 1,000 feet, the officer tail gunner reported less than half of the eighteen Forts in formation.

The route out had us zigzagging from one point to another as we climbed, with certain tracks designated for forming with the other two air groups of eighteen in order to complete the wing combat box of fifty-four. Spares tagged along to take the place of any ships that had to abort. But all this complicated flying also required good weather. I knew we'd never get formed by following the plan and that I'd have to find a clear area between cloud decks and circle there. This would require breaking radio silence. It was either that or abort the whole mission.

I radioed to the lost aircraft of my eighteen-plane formation to join me over point A at 3,000 feet. When I got there I found solid soup. So I canceled those orders and announced we would assemble over point B at 5,000 feet. By now the radio channels were filled with grumbles and griping, pilots talking to each other and trying to get fixes. I had to repeat instructions to the Cowboys (our call sign) several times to get through.

At point B a few stray birds tacked on to our formation, but the clouds were still too thick for any reasonable assembly. On studying the sky I realized I'd have to climb to 10,000 feet to get in the clear. That would be 4,000 above our planned departure altitude, and it would waste precious gas. I told the Cowboys that I'd circle over Splasher 4 (a radio beacon) at ten angles firing red flares. Up we went and I could almost feel the fuel pouring into our laboring engines. On arrival over the splasher we found the air filled with a vast whirlpool of circling bombers. Other groups had, of course, run into the same problem.

Our engineer fired red flares as fast as he could from the top turret. After two great circles, losing more fuel and setting our timing back by at least twenty minutes, the tail gunner counted a box of fifty Forts tacked onto us, including strays from three other groups. That was enough to go to war, and we headed out over the North Sea into clear air. The surface sparkled in the brilliant sunlight.

Already I was planning how to shorten our return route. Only that way would we have enough fuel to complete the mission. If we followed the planned return route we'd be ditching in the North Sea.

Mission strategy was to cross the Jutland peninsula at its base near Kiel. There we were to rendezvous with P-47s from VIII Fighter Command, who would give us cover over the crossing as we proceeded east.

We expected the Luftwaffe to concentrate its whole force there to ambush us on withdrawal. There'd be plenty of time for the Jerries to assemble there. Consequently, it was planned that on return we would recross the peninsula a hundred miles north of Kiel and throw the enemy off balance. But now that northern withdrawal route was out of the question. We wouldn't have enough fuel. We'd have to return on the reciprocal of our penetration track and run the gauntlet.

I passed this on to Bob Chapin who, with his assistant,

began to work out new withdrawal tracks and figure fuel consumption. Even doing it this way it would be a tight squeeze. I instructed our radio operator to inform Eighth Air Force in code of my intentions, hoping they would dispatch all the fighters available to help us recross Denmark.

We put on oxygen masks, flak vests, parachutes, and helmets as we climbed slowly to 12,000 feet. The tail gunner reported that he could see three other wing boxes behind us. I knew many outfits couldn't get formed and had to abort the mission, and I had no idea how large the total force was. But with at least four wings in the stream, things were picking up. The gunners test-fired their .50s. We were ready.

Being about forty minutes late at the planned rendezvous with Vinegrove (our Little Friends), we missed them altogether. But, wonder of wonders, we didn't see a single enemy fighter as we sailed across the peninsula. (I learned later that those wings behind us didn't have it as lucky and got into lively scraps with enemy fighters.) Weaving our way through some sporadic flak we continued out over the Baltic.

The weather remained crystal clear as I watched surface ships zigzagging below us, leaving curved white wakes. "We're not after you," I thought. "We're after much bigger game. We don't launch hundreds of warplanes to bomb a few nondescript freighters."

Sweden loomed in the distant mist to our left as we droned steadily deeper into enemy territory. We made landfall near Danzig after climbing to 15,000 feet, our bombing altitude. This was going to be a piece of cake. Hermann the German would be surprised to find us hunting him so far east of Berlin.

Marienburg materialized just as briefed, along with the doomed aircraft assembly plant and airdrome. My three groups took intervals for separate bombing. Each would salvo on the leader's bombs as they left his bomb bay. Bombardier Dick Crown took control of our eighteen-plane box and lived up to his deadeye reputation. The tail gunner reported solid hits on all aiming points, and I hoped we had caught fat Hermann outside his shelter. (After studying subsequent recce photos, Eighth Air Force reported results of the bombing "good to excellent.")

There was some scattered and very inaccurate flak on the wing assembly after bombs away. Bursts dirtied the sky as much as half a mile behind us. I laughed over the radio. "Hah! They must have the Home Guard manning those guns!" At this point we hadn't lost a single Fort.

Back again over the quiet Baltic, two B-17s peeled off from our formation and headed toward Sweden. All props were turning, and I suspected they had found a good way to resign from the war. Rumor had it that the Swedes provided luxurious accommodations for interned crews. I was somewhat relieved to note that neither Fort had the 384th triangle "P" on its fin. I yelled at them to get back in formation, but there was no answer as they faded into the distance. To give them the benefit of the doubt, they could have been so low on fuel that they did not want to risk ditching. But they should have told me that.

Chapin came on the interphone to say that we had enough fuel to make it to England, but just. He doubted that following aircraft would all make it to base, however, and suggested that we make landfall at Great Yarmouth, the nearest English turf. An RAF base was nearby. That sounded like good thinking. If my fuel was low the others were bound to be in worse shape, because more fuel is consumed by flying formation than by leading. It's the frequent jockeying of the throttles that draws down the gas while the leader can fly at a constant throttle setting.

By now we were approaching Kiel, and there were other things to think about. The whole Luftwaffe seemed to be lying in wait for us. We began to take quartering and head-on attacks from flights of two to six, and our responding guns shook *Screaming Eagle* and thundered over the engine roar. Our box formation of forty-eight tightened up like magic for mutual protection, each pilot getting as close as he dared to his leader. My heart sank. Had we used up our good luck?

But no! Gen. Jimmy Doolittle had not been asleep. Suddenly the tables were turned. The general had dispatched almost every fighter in England to rendezvous with us at the base of the peninsula. The skies erupted with Little Friends diving out of the low western sun, like the U.S. Cavalry coming to the rescue. It was a donnybrook the likes of which I had never seen. There were no more Luftwaffe attacks on us. German airmen were fighting for their lives, and losing. The sky was lit by one exploding fighter after another.

Almost everywhere I looked there were vicious dogfights in progress. I even saw Little Friends fighting with their droptanks still on. I supposed they wanted to stay in the fray as long as possible and run up their scores. I remarked to myself, "This is the greatest show on earth!" Then the afterthought: "But the price of admission is too high." I was awed at the grandeur and heroism of this great aerial battle that left our bomber wing unscathed. Never did I more love and respect our Little Friends.

Within twenty minutes we had passed beyond the battle and found the North Sea beneath us. Now came the frantic and forlorn calls from one pilot after another. "We're low on gas." "Don't think we can make it." "What'll we do?"

Chapin already had us on course to the nearest landfall. Then with the help of our engineer we figured the lowest possible RPM, manifold pressure, and fuel mixture settings and passed this data to the other aircraft. Putting *Screaming Eagle* in a slightly descending attitude, we were able to stay in the air at a very slow speed, consuming minimum fuel. Next I ordered all aircraft short of fuel to lighten their loads—to throw out guns and ammo and to drop the heavy ball turrets.

Then I prayed.

It took more than two hours to transit the North Sea. I

intercepted Maydays from two ships from other wings. They were ditching and gave their positions, which I relayed to Eighth Air Force. The sun had set before our straining eyes sighted land. Clouds had lifted over England, and within minutes we found the Royal Air Force station at Norwich. Everyone landed. We had been airborne twelve hours, and had flown sixteen hundred miles. No one had had to ditch, and none had been shot down. Only the two who had gone to Sweden were missing. But the 384th didn't get back to Grafton Underwood until the next day, after enjoying the warm RAF hospitality.

"Report of Operations, 9 April 1944" by the Eighth Air Force shows two combat wings of the 1st Bomb Division, 41A and 41B, attacking the Marienburg targets. Only three losses were indicated, which means the following wing lost one. Sadly this was a 384th Fort that had tacked on to 41B. However, because of the mixture of Forts from several groups in each air wing and because many had landed away from home base, it is doubtful that the official report is very accurate.

Wings bombing other targets suffered worse than 41A and 41B. A total of thirty-two bombers were lost, thirteen from "unknown causes." Some of these must have ended in the cold North Sea. Oddly, no mention of this is in the official report. Nor is there any note of the sweat we had with fuel consumption. I suppose the staff officers who wrote the report didn't consider this too significant.

14

Oberpfaffenhofen

The Ops planners of the Eighth Air Force had decided to try a new tactic on the raid of April 24 against the Dornier-Werke G.m.b.H. and Factory Airfield at Oberpfaffenhofen. This was a big fighter assembly facility and one of the POINTBLANK targets. Extra B-17s and crews were continuing to pour into England from the Zone of the Interior (ZI), and we'd become strong enough for each numbered combat wing to put up two air wings of fifty-four B-17s each. So the Ops people had decided to penetrate with the two large formations flying abreast, called "A" and "B" wings. That way, they reasoned, we would expose ourselves to flak and fighters for a shorter period of time. In other words, it would cut the length of our bomber stream in half. It seemed reasonable enough, but there were some hidden hookers.

General Travis was to lead the 41A wing as well as to command both formations of 41A and 41B—a total of 108 Forts carrying about a thousand airmen. Bob Travis was, in fact, the leader of the whole Eighth Air Force that day, some eight hundred bombers and perhaps half that many escort fighters, but his duties in this capacity amounted only to a decision whether to carry on or to abort the mission—and the Eighth Air Force never aborted unless the weather got really stinking.

The luck of the draw, depending how one looked at it, gave me the lead of the 41B wing. I was ordered to fly on the right of 41A and dress left on it. Then, as we approached the target, I was to slide 41B in behind 41A and ahead of the "A" wing of the following outfit. At the briefing this sounded easy.

It was a beautiful day and we assembled without difficulty. Passing west of London we were at 16,000 feet on departing England at Beachy Head. Our double wings penetrated the French coast twenty minutes later at 20,000 feet amid a shower of flak. There we turned left 16 degrees and I had my first indication that something was wrong. I found my wing somewhat behind 41A of General Travis. He slowed down some, and I increased indicated airspeed from 152 to 155 mph. Soon we were lined up like West Pointers passing in review.

A squadron leader had been mortally hit by flak at the French coast but his deputy had promptly assumed command and we were in pretty good shape. About a hundred miles east of Paris we made another left turn, this time 30 degrees. It became apparent then that the wings-abreast idea was seriously flawed. When we completed the turn I found myself miles behind 41A. In fact I was even behind the "A" wing of the following formations.

Bob Travis called to me to dress up and I increased speed to 158 mph indicated, which was about the maximum for a fifty-four-airplane gaggle of B-17s, and even then some birds began to straggle. But there was no catching up. A third turn to the left of 26 degrees near Strasbourg cracked the whip again, aggravating my problem. Those on the outside of my wing began to drop back dangerously. It was an invitation to enemy fighters and they accepted it.

For over an hour we had flown across France with little or no opposition. But this all changed as we headed into Germany. South of Stuttgart enemy aircraft, sometimes six or nine abreast, were vectored in on our noses. They came in waves, firing headlight ammunition that sparkled like rain in the sun. It seemed impossible to avoid this hail of fire as hundreds of rounds flew directly at us. Of course our B-17s suffered much battle damage, but they could take a lot and still fly. Nevertheless, three of them went down under this withering assault. I had cut the speed to a respectable 150 to allow the stragglers to rejoin the formation, but they hadn't caught up when the fighters hit.

I abandoned any thought of dressing on 41A. We were far behind and the parade of "A" wings on my left were jammed together as closely as a queue at a London bus stop. There certainly was no room for me to slip in behind 41A.

The plan had been to fly north of Munich and then circle around to the right. Theoretically this should have cracked the whip in the opposite direction, opening up the interval between the "A" wings on my left and permitting the "B" wings to slide in behind for the bombing. But at this point the formations were so badly scrambled that an on-the-spot correction was called for. The big fifty-four-plane formations were simply too unwieldy to do what the Ops planners had in mind.

I knew Bob Travis couldn't see the deplorable condition of the formations behind him. All he could see was how badly disorganized my 41B was, and he let me know it over the radio in no uncertain terms.

Radio traffic was a tower of babble. Not only were the Germans attempting to jam our frequency with their "mad fiddler," but it seemed as if everyone was calling for help as the enemy fighters took large bites out of our formations. At the first attack I had called for "Balance-one," the leader's call sign of our fighter escort that was supposed to have been in the Augsburg-Munich area.

"Balance-one" finally responded through the radio noise (part of which was caused by the angry calls of General Travis ordering me to straighten out my formation and dress up).

"Balance-one" assured me his fighters were on the way. The Little Friends protected some of the following wings, but never got to the front of the column where the heavy action was. My wing lost two more Forts north of Munich and others were badly shot up.

Being unable to slide in behind 41A, the option open to me was obvious, but it would require an act of insubordination. I could turn my 41B to the right before General Travis turned 41A, bombing the target first.

I knew Bob Travis prized his position at the head of the bomber stream. He would be the first over the target and have an unobstructed view of it, while the following formations would have to bomb through the smoke and debris caused by earlier bomb explosions. Taking the brunt of the fighter attack, the lead wing certainly deserved that advantage. I knew he wouldn't look kindly on my move, no matter how logical.

Perhaps I could have S-ed to slow our advance and looked for an opening somewhere back in the parade of "A" wings, but that would have taken the position of some other "B" wing. Besides, it would have exposed my wing unnecessarily to more flak and fighters. Our losses at this point were prohibitive, principally because I had tried to follow orders and stay abreast. The integrity of my wing had been almost lost before I cut the speed back. And I was condemning myself bitterly for having acted like a cadet. No, I decided, we'd go in first. To hell with what General Travis might do.

Augsburg and Munich loomed through camouflage smoke off my right wing and I knew Oberpfaffenhofen was almost due south of Munich. As we drew beyond the metropolis I began to wheel the big forty-nine–ship 41B formation around to the right, starting the circle of the city well outside the flak envelope. A scream penetrated the babble of radio voices and I knew who it was. I didn't intend to respond. I was committed. There was nothing else to do but go ahead with my plan of taking the lead. So, like Lord Nelson at the battle of Copenhagen when he put the spyglass to his blind eye and thus couldn't see the signal to retreat, I turned off my radio.

The Luftwaffe hit us again just before the IP. They were viciously flying through their own flak. My hot bombardier, Dick Crown, and methodical navigator, Bob Chapin, were busy working out the attack strategy and were unable to respond with the nose guns. I wished that I had some fixed guns I could fire from the cockpit like a fighter. It was a helpless feeling watching all that sparkling ammunition flying at us.

Another 41B went down. The low group leader was badly hit but continued in formation. I couldn't see it but my officer tail gunner kept me informed. (I wished that Bob Travis had used this system of having an experienced pilot ride in the tail. So far as I knew the 384th was the only group to practice it.)

By now our formation had closed up and the three eighteen-plane groups (or what was left of them) took interval smartly for the bomb run. Each group was to bomb separately on the signal of its lead bombardier—that signal being the leader's bombs leaving his bomb bay. Only the lead group bombardier handled the bombsight, the following planes simply toggling off their bombs. This tactic had four advantages. First, the best bombardiers of the groups would do the bomb aiming for everyone. Second, a tighter pattern of bombs would smother the target. Third, the bombing operation could be carried out more rapidly than if each ship bombed individually, hence less exposure to flak. And finally, the groups would retain a defensive formation of supporting fire in the event of fighter attack.

We had flown straight and level for eight minutes to permit the bombardier to crank in drift and stabilize the cross hairs on the Norden sight. Ed Ulrey switched to automatic pilot and gave control of the airplane to Dick Crown in the nose. Bob Chapin, as usual, had done a masterful job of navigating, and the large German aircraft assembly plant was clearly visible ahead as we slowly—too slowly!—crept up on it.

Flak peppered us unmercifully, but there could be no evasive action. It seemed that Hitler had no intention of letting us destroy this vital manufacturing facility. For the first time on the mission I had nothing to do but sit and watch the awesome drama of soaring Forts running the gauntlet of deadly flak. At every burst I flinched mentally. I admired my skillful pilot, Ed Ulrey, who calmly monitored the instruments as if he were driving down Broadway. When the flak got thick, I liked to do the flying, but that was impossible on this interminable bomb run. Explosions rocked our tormented B-17, and fragments of flak rattled on its skin. One spent hunk of metal came through the side next to me and hit my seat.

The eight-minute run seemed an eternity. Finally, the more-than-welcome "Bombs away!" came from Crown in the nose accompanied by a slight lurch upward as our ship loosed its load of 500-pounders.

Ed Ulrey coolly snapped off the autopilot and took the wheel. With hand signals I directed him to bank left and let down. Now we could maneuver to spoil the aim of the ground gunners.

I had turned the radio back on and mercifully heard no more from General Travis. A call came from my right wingman. "Cowboy leader, you're losing fuel."

Plastering my head against the right window I could see a misty spray of fluid leaving engine three. It would just be a matter of moments, I thought, before it would catch fire and we blew up. I had seen it happen to others.

Jerking off my oxygen mask, I sniffed the air; there was no odor of gas. It had to be hydraulic fluid. What a relief! I replaced my mask and passed the good word to our crew, who were preparing to bail out. For the moment we were safe.

Forming back into a combat wing box, we led the Eighth Air Force on the withdrawal from Germany and across France. Two badly crippled Forts had to peel off just after "bombs away" and head for Switzerland. We never heard from them again, and were later told that they had been shot down by the Swiss Air Force. One of the Forts was copiloted by Floyd Edwards, whose wedding I had attended only a week before.*

My worries weren't over. First, we had to land without a hydraulic system; that meant no flaps and no brakes. And in those days there was no barrier at the end of the runway. To top it off we found a Fort burning in the middle of the landing strip. I hoped the crew had escaped.

It looked like we might have to ground loop in order to stop on the airfield. I had had some experience landing a Fort with neither brakes nor flaps, and took the wheel from Ed. Coming in low just above a stall, we put it down on the grass over the fence, pointing at the longest diagonal possible. As our speed bled off, we headed toward a distant hardstand and used the last few feet of its taxi strip to roll to a stop.

Tom Beckett in a jeep had followed the fire and meat wagons that had chased us. He brought the bad news I expected.

"General Travis wants to see you in his office immediately!"

As soon as I could shuck off my flying gear I climbed into my beat-up staff car and told Sergeant Montgomery to drive me the twelve miles to headquarters of the 41st Wing. It was like riding a tumbril to my execution. Certainly my days of command were over. I would lose my group just as it was climbing out of its earlier depression. I might even be court-martialed.

General Travis was steaming with anger when I reported and saluted, but he was compassionate enough to direct me toward a chair. No doubt he was as bushed as I was. I suffered his tirade until he had wound down, reasoning that my best ap-

---

* Some forty years later I ran into Floyd Clinton Edwards, alive and kicking, at a 384th reunion.

proach was not to contradict or even comment until he had dispelled some of his wrath. Then I might be permitted to tell the whole story as I saw it. At last he asked me to explain my insubordination.

As carefully as I could, I explained how the left turns across France had caused the outside wings to crack the whip, and how I had increased speed to catch up; how this had strung out my wing and made it vulnerable to fighters; how I had cut back my speed to preserve the defensive formation; and how it had become impossible to slide my wing in behind him because of the jamming together of the "A" wings on the left.

Using my hands to illustrate the wings-abreast turns I showed him that my only logical course of action was to assume the lead on the right turn around Munich and I apologized for having to upstage him. Then I condemned the wings-abreast tactic as unworkable. (Incidently, it was never tried again with these large wing boxes.)

Bob Travis listened to it all. I have to hand it to him; he was fair and reasonable and didn't hold a grudge. Disappointed as he was with the heavy losses his wing took, he evidently decided it wasn't my fault and that I'd taken the only reasonable course of action. Suddenly his expression softened, and for a long moment he regarded the pencil with which he had been taking notes.

"Yes," he finally said resignedly in a low voice. "I guess you did the right thing. Okay," he brightened, "I want you to put yourself in for a Silver Star."

"I can't do that, General," I protested. "That's your responsibility."

"Do it!" he commanded.

And that was another order I disobeyed. I never did get that Silver Star, but a more appropriate award came out of the Oberpfaffenhofen mission. The 384th Bomb Group was given another Presidential Unit Citation.

My records show that the 384th Bomb Group contributed thirty B-17s to the original 41B air wing of fifty-four. The 303rd put up twenty-four Forts to fill out the 41B formation. My records don't indicate the 303rd losses, but Roger A. Freeman's book, *The Mighty Eighth*, notes that 41B lost fifteen Forts altogether.

Of the thirty we put up, seven were lost over Germany. Four others that made it back to England had killed and wounded aboard, and two landed at Boxted, unable to make it home to Grafton Underwood.

It seemed to me that the only good thing about the show was that we hit the target squarely. Dick Crown had done it again, and we had slowed the manufacture of enemy fighters. Postwar evidence, however, showed that this aspect of POINT-BLANK wasn't too significant, because German fighter production increased despite our bombing of their manufacturing facilities. What the mission did do was to demonstrate once again to Germany that their all-out defenses could not stop the Eighth from penetrating deep into Germany and bombing any target successfully. In this sense the Luftwaffe was defeated. It had committed dozens of Stürmgruppen especially designed to knock down heavy bombers with head-on attacks of up to thirty fighters. But the tactic was largely broken up by our escort fighters and the withering fire from the guns of the heavy bombers. During the month of April, although we lost over five hundred aircraft, Eighth Air Force claimed over a thousand enemy fighters shot down. General Spaatz's strategy was paying off.

We didn't have a chance to lick our wounds. Next day we bombed a Luftwaffe airfield in France and two days later we bombed three more. We finished out the month of April with another Berlin mission on the twenty-ninth, flying a thirty-six-plane wing.

We flew thirteen missions in April 1944, taking more losses

than we had in any other month of the war. We had flown to that Eighth Air Force nemesis, Schweinfurt, on the thirteenth, and lost nine planes. I grieved for the missing crews and for the dead and wounded brought home. And I worried that the group might again feel sorry for itself. But my worries were groundless. Oddly, our esprit de corps had reached a high plateau. We were hitting our targets and fighting through no matter what the sacrifices. Other groups respected us, and the high command knew it could count on us, knew we would bounce back from a rough mission and carry on.

15

R.H.I.P.

While all this was going on, I had complained to the Division G-4 about the condition of the two staff cars assigned to the 384th, a Plymouth sedan long overdue for the junk heap and a Ford about as roadworthy. One or the other was usually in the shop, sometimes both.

Vehicle accidents were common. All of our vehicles were of American design with left-hand steering wheels, and to pass a car ahead in left-hand traffic one had to swing far out in the right lane to see if there were any oncoming cars. Sometimes it was a dangerous maneuver. Moreover, it took our drivers several weeks to get used to left-hand traffic. It wasn't for nothing that British cars had right-hand drives.

Considering the many meetings I had to attend away from Grafton Underwood, I wanted something more reliable. That was the argument I used in my official requisition for new staff cars, but I also admitted that I wanted transportation more befitting a full colonel commanding a combat group. Quite frankly, I was embarrassed to be riding in one of these dilapidated jalopies, like some laborer headed for a construction job. The other group commanders I knew all had spiffy new sedans.

My requisitions were returned disapproved. According to the Division G-4 there were no better staff cars available in all of

England, and I'd have to get along with what I had. I noted ironically that Division and Eighth Air Force headquarters were not hurting for good staff cars.

One rainy day when I was on a forty-eight-hour pass, and Bob Montgomery was driving me around London, I happened to remark, "Where are all the private cars in England? I never see any."

"They were all impounded after the Blitz," Bob said. "A move to save gasoline."

"Wonder what the government did with them," I said.

"Might be interesting to find out," Bob mused. "Why don't we try?"

"Why not? I understand there're some important British headquarters in Grosvenor Square. Let's go there and ask some questions."

"Yes, Sir!" Bob responded with enthusiasm as he turned the old Plymouth in that direction.

It was no trouble finding a parking place in Grosvenor Square, which was surrounded by imposing old office buildings. Bob went one way and I another, meeting back at the car in twenty minutes. He should have been a private eye. "It's over there in that building," Bob pointed. "An office on the top floor handles all the impounded cars."

The hardest part of the exercise was climbing the four flights of stairs. There we found a sparse, closet-size office, smelling of ancient rotting wood and manned by an elderly British Army major and an orderly. I explained that we had an old Plymouth sedan and wondered if it would be possible to trade it for one of the impounded cars.

The major was a man of action. He selected a yellow slip of paper, scribbled on it, and handed it to me.

"Tyke this to the address on the slip. The vehicles are in a warehouse there."

Bob found the warehouse on the edge of town and we

surrendered the yellow slip to the man in charge. "Just leave your old vehicle here," he said, "and tyke your pick of those in the warehouse."

I was astonished. "You mean any car here?" The warehouse bulged with beautiful rolling stock like a grand auto show.

"That's right. Any machine. Tyke your pick."

The vast building held every conceivable kind of automobile, old and new, big and small. Bob found an imposing black Packard sedan that some earl or duke must have contributed to the war effort. It glowed with a patina on its surface that suggested countless polishings by a uniformed chauffeur. There was even a coat of arms on a door. "Let's take this, Colonel," he urged.

"You know how long we'd be able to keep that? Within twenty-four hours some general would take it from us. Pick out something more modest, more befitting a colonel's transportation."

Bob selected an almost new 1939 Studebaker President sedan. It had a striking maroon finish, with a motor that purred like a pussycat. And, of course, the safer right-hand drive. We returned to Grafton Underwood in style. At every stop Bob was out with a rag polishing the handsome car.

Not many days later Bob came to me with a reasonable request. Would I let him take the old Ford down to that treasure trove of impounded cars and exchange it for something better? I told him to go ahead. "But don't bring back that Packard," I cautioned. "It'd be a waste of time."

You guessed it. Grinning from ear to ear, Bob proudly drove up to our headquarters the next day with that block-long ebony Packard.

Not long after that, General Travis and staff visited us to challenge my headquarters to a game of volleyball. On one of the breaks Travis sidled up to me and whispered, "What general is on the base, Dale?"

"You're the only general here, General."

"Then whose car is that?" he pointed at the Packard.

"That's mine, General," I said, modestly blowing on my fingernails and polishing them on my shirt.

R.H.I.P., as they say—rank has its privileges. Bob Travis drove home in the Packard. But he left me his big Chrysler sedan. Not many days later a staff general from Division spied the Chrysler and traded me his almost-new Ford sedan for it. At least we ended up with two good cars, and Bob Montgomery became reconciled to driving the maroon Studebaker President. I believe he even grew to love it, for he polished that maroon finish almost down to the bare metal.

One day at a staff meeting we were talking about those devastating head-on attacks the Jerries were using. They came at us in flights of six to twelve in formation, obviously vectored to a head-on attack by ground radar. The closing speed approached 800 mph. Almost before we could charge our guns the tiny specks ahead grew to aircraft spouting a withering fire of 20-mm exploding shells.

It was a helpless feeling for a pilot to have to sit there and endure this hot rain of fire with nothing much to do about it but pray, particularly in the case of leaders. Their navigators and bombardiers in the greenhouses were too busy to shoot back with the two .50s in the chin turret. I made the offhand remark that it would be nice if the lead pilot had a button on the wheel that would fire fixed guns like a fighter plane.

This remark was overheard by Capt. Nathan Mazer, my gung ho armament officer. Before many days had passed he asked me to look at a B-17 he had modified. The chin turret had been removed and six fixed .50-caliber guns bristled in its place. Nate showed me how all the guns could be fired simultaneously by pressing a button on the pilot's wheel.

I told him it looked deadly, and suggested we take it up to The Wash and test it on some whitecaps.

Nate flew in the nose to charge the guns and be sure they all fired properly, while I had a picnic aiming the big B-17 at whitecaps. The six .50s put out so much firepower that the whitecaps were churned with the hail of bullets, and it was easy to aim. I resolved to take it on my next mission.

Before my turn to lead came up, however, that ship was assigned to one of the squadron leaders and was shot down. So much for the B-17 fighter. By then, however, I was carrying an assistant navigator in the nose, and he was able to man the chin turret while the group navigator and bombardier were doing their paperwork and bombsighting.

Eventually I concluded that fixed nose guns fired by the pilot wasn't a very practical solution after all. The lead ship couldn't jink around to aim the guns without messing up the formation he was leading and possibly throwing off the bomb aiming. Anyway, attacks by enemy aircraft were becoming less frequent. Our long-range escort fighters, P-51 Mustangs, P-47 Jugs (officially called Thunderbolts, but we called them Jugs because that was what they looked like), and P-38 Lightnings, were winning the air battle over Germany.

This fact came vividly to my attention one day as we withdrew across France from a mission to Frankfurt. Our escort had left us for more action elsewhere. Only one ME-109 appeared. It didn't attack but flew formation with me at three o'clock low, just out of range of our guns. Yet it was almost near enough to see the expressions on the German pilot's face. It was very odd, indeed, his flying along with us like that. He seemed to be in good shape; there was no battle damage that I could see, and his prop was turning over nicely. No smoke was coming from his engine. What was he doing there, flying formation with me?

The Luftwaffe pilot must have held that position for ten minutes or more. He didn't wave or make any sign; he just stuck there out of range. Then all of a sudden he jettisoned his canopy, stood up, and bailed out. He had obviously decided to take his chances in occupied France, rather than continue the war as a fighter pilot.

The thought struck me like a flash of lightning—*we had won the war!* Yes, by God, we had won. I was sure of it. If the morale of a fighter pilot had reached such depths it was pretty obvious that the entire Luftwaffe was becoming afflicted with the dread virus of defeat. Oh, there would be plenty of fighting left and much blood spilled before Hitler gave up, but the issue was no longer in doubt. It was just a matter of continuing to pound the Reich until Hitler said "uncle."

It was pretty obvious that we had control of the air over *Festung Europa.* Soon we would wear the Luftwaffe down to complete impotence. Then we could systematically destroy the essential industries of the Reich: aircraft production, rail transportation, petroleum resources, submarine production, and whatever else Germany needed to survive as a viable country. We could lay on an air siege and keep squeezing the German economy until Hitler would have to sue for peace.

Meanwhile a vast Allied armada was gathering in the ports of southern England, preparing to launch the greatest invasion of history. It was no secret that our cross-channel attack would come sometime this summer. Just when and where was the big secret. Allied planners had no faith that air power could win the war alone. Waiting out an air siege would be too indefinite. Moreover, Churchill and Roosevelt were being hounded by Stalin to establish a second front and siphon off some of the pressure on troops from the eastern front. A clear military victory on the ground, as in World War I, was the objective of the Allied leaders.

D day was nearing and we were often being sent out to bomb railway marshaling yards in order to throw a block into German logistics. I led the 41st Wing on May 9 to attack the railway yards at Thionville, France. Our bombing accuracy was only fair, but otherwise the mission was run without a hitch. There were no aborts and no losses. In fact, except at the enemy coast, there was no flak. Truly a piece of cake.

On May 27 I led the wing again against marshaling yards at Mannheim, Germany, a considerably deeper penetration than the Thionville raid. This was my seventeenth mission. Our group put up a total of thirty-eight Forts. There was one abort caused by the failure of a fuel valve, but no losses. We made a shambles of the railway yards and witnessed a fierce battle between our escort fighters and the Luftwaffe, but no enemy aircraft attacked us. Things were picking up for the 384th. We were graduating from being a good group to a great group.

On the way home from Mannheim I urged the squadrons to tighten up their formations and complimented them on a real showcase mission.

"This is Cowboy leader. Good show, Cowboys. Ride 'em, Cowboys! Check in."

"Cowboy red, roger."

"Cowboy blue, roger dodger."

"Cowboy white, roger dodger Old Codger."

A smile split my face under the oxygen mask. My boys were beginning to feel proud of themselves, and confident enough even to kid the Old Man. Yes, the 384th was riding high.

Some months earlier the 384th had been assigned the dubious honor of trying out the first guided missiles in combat. Our bomb dump was bulging with glide bombs, GB-1s. These were 2,000-pound bombs with stubby wings that were to be released from our Forts several miles short of the target and then they would glide in. The technicians who had designed this weapon assured us the bombs could easily hit a city the size of Dayton, Ohio. Moreover, our Forts could avoid the heavy flak found around German targets.

We in the Eighth were wedded to the concept of precision bombing of military installations and key industries. Although the Royal Air Force had long practiced area bombing of German cities at night, few of the American leaders in England approved of this strategy. Consequently, the use of glide bombs, which could not be aimed accurately enough to strike a point target, and were area weapons, was opposed by Jimmy Doolittle. But he had his orders. The chair-borne leaders in Washington insisted that we give the contraptions a try.

We practiced releasing these glide bombs, which were code named "Grapefruit," over The Wash, and were not too unhappy to learn that at our usual formation speed of about 155 mph indicated airspeed, the bombs wouldn't glide at all but tumbled into the sea. It was several months before word came back from Washington that we should dive the Forts to pick up an airspeed of about 175 mph. Then, said the engineers at Wright Field, the GB-1s would fly. Of course the engineers knew little about handling a formation of thirty-six or more B-17s, or even a group of twelve. Diving them would be a very sporty tactic, indeed.

But we had dragged our feet long enough, and on May 28, 1944, we were ordered out to attack Cologne with glide bombs. I rode along on this mission to see how it would work. We took interval with air groups of twelve, dove until we registered 180 mph, leveled off to let our speed bleed off to 175, and then released the glide bombs. By that time our formations were pretty ragged.

Although our bombardiers had followed their instructions to the letter, not a single glide bomb fell in Cologne. Jerry flak gunners put in many claims for B-17s shot down, when all that happened was a rain of exploding glide bombs littering the countryside. The engineers at Wright Field continued to design improved models of the GB-1, but we were never again ordered to test them.

Although my problems at Grafton Underwood were being resolved, my problems in New York were growing worse. The news from home was very disturbing. On May 8, Alice Bucknam, Ralph Bucknam's sister who lived in Freeport, Long Island, wrote me a letter from the hospital at Mitchel Field where Elise was a patient. Elise was suffering from a serious concussion, and was unable to write, she reported, but could dictate some of the letter. About two weeks earlier, Alice wrote, Elise had been driving across the Queensboro Bridge in the evening with a friend when a truck cut in front of them and they crashed against the bridge supports. Details of the accident were sketchy, and all Alice knew was that Elise had been unconscious for some time before being brought to Mitchel. The doctors said that she'd have to remain in the hospital for at least three more weeks, but her prognosis was good.

Alice assured me that Kort and Voan were being well-cared-for by an excellent nurse, a Mrs. Ehrhart, and soon I received other letters confirming this.

There wasn't much I could do other than send cables, flowers, write comforting letters, and bite my fingernails. Elise seemed to have suffered one crisis after another since I had left New York. When she was finally able to write on the fifteenth, the letter rambled and shed little light on her condition or the accident. She said she had been unconscious from April 24 to May 8, the day Alice visited her and wrote the letter.

Alice wrote that Elise had been admitted to the Mitchel Field hospital on April 30. Where had she been for the week after the accident? And who had admitted her to the hospital? It all sounded odd and more serious than the letters implied. I knew I wasn't getting the whole story. Elise did mention that someone named Frank Fleet was riding with her when the accident occurred. This was the first I had heard of him. Who was he?

This disturbing news from home drove me into a mean depression, and I fear I was too hard on the few men who had screwed up on missions. Copies of messages I sent to the air and ground execs and to the squadron commanders reveal an unforgiving sharpness and arbitrary directions for "corrective action." I was still hammering on the pilots to fly closer formations, and although their performance had improved markedly I was never satisfied.

This touchiness was carried over into other activities, and is illustrated by an incident that occurred one evening when I visited Bill Gross at Bassingbourn. Bill lived in a bachelor apartment, a brick building that was the envy of all those of us who lived in temporary Quonset huts. When I knocked at his door (the Brits called this "knocking someone up," a phrase that always brought smiles to us Yanks) a civilian answered: a particularly handsome, well-built young man. He introduced me to another one of his kind there and explained that they, too, were waiting for General Gross.

I soon learned that these two very healthy young men were tennis players who had been sent by the War Department to entertain the troops. I imagine Bassingbourn was the only USAAF air patch in England that had a tennis court, so of course that was their destination. As we talked I grew more and more incensed that these two athletes could avoid the draft by playing tennis for the troops. Thoughts of the heavy losses of fine young American boys flashed through my mind. And here were two draft-dodgers being sent around the world at government expense to play tennis!

When I learned that these two had not yet met Bill Gross, and that they had rudely invited themselves into Bill's quarters—simply walked in as if it were a public office—I lost my temper. Anger so arose in my throat that I nearly choked.

"You mean you entered General Gross's quarters without being invited?" I accused.

"The door was open."

"That makes no difference. These are his private quarters and I suggest you leave immediately."

They hesitated, so I opened the door and threw each one

into the hall. Perhaps they could sense that I was ready to kill them and they put up no resistance.

We flew thirty-six missions in May. When we put up more than one group we were credited for two missions. We did this fifteen times that month. Most of the targets were in France; we struck railway marshaling yards, Luftwaffe airfields, buzz bomb sites, and artillery emplacements in the Pas de Calais. I was convinced that the Pas de Calais was where the landing would take place, and so were Adolf Hitler and his Wehrmacht staff generals in Berlin. But not Field Marshal Erwin Rommel, who had been given command of all the forces that were to repel the invasion, the Atlantic Wall. *Der Führer* fancied himself a great strategist, and his toadying chief of staff, Alfred Jodl, went along with the fixation that the invasion would come against the Calais beaches. Hitler personally held two crack Panzer divisions there, believing that was where Patton's army would invade, even after the incontrovertible evidence was in that our major assault was at the landings in Normandy. Part of this gigantic and successful spoof was caused by our repeated bombing of the Calais targets.

We knew the invasion was imminent. The Eighth Air Force had been taken off the strategic bombing mission and was responding to the tactical needs of Gen. Dwight D. Eisenhower. The French targets were not as well defended as those in Germany and our losses were minimal, but it was no free ride, and now and then a flak burst would knock down one of our Forts.

One warm afternoon I watched the 384th prepare to launch a raid on the two great dirigible hangars at Orly Airport just outside of Paris. Intelligence told us that the Luftwaffe was using the hangars to repair battle-damaged fighters. Suddenly I got the urge to see Paris, my last visit there having been in the summer of 1934 when I went on a cruise with the Midshipmen of Annapolis. But it was too late to take the lead with *Screaming Eagle*.

Anyway, it was about time I eyeballed a 384th war formation for myself. I had often imagined how much one could see from the tail gunner's position. There one would have a view of the forming of squadrons, groups, and wings, and a clear picture of the bomb drop and explosions on the ground. None of this could be seen by the pilots of the lead ship, who got their information secondhand from the tail gunner.

We were now flying a thirty-six-plane wing box instead of the fifty-four-plane formation. This much more maneuverable unit had adequate defensive firepower to defend itself against a Luftwaffe subdued by our aggressive Little Friends. With the flood of new aircraft and crews from the States, each bomb group could now put up its own wing box of thirty-six. The general configuration of the box formation was much the same as before, with a lead squadron of twelve, another squadron of twelve high and to the left, and a low squadron of twelve to the right, all three being staggered so as not to be abreast of any other.

I suspected my troops would regard my decision to ride in the tail on this mission as an anomie, or perhaps a grandstand play, and a chance to chalk up another mission on a milk run. But the more I thought of it the more sense it made, and I wondered if I could fit my long frame into that confined space. Perhaps it would give me a better understanding of what the tail gunner endured, and I might even get a chance to shoot at a bogey or two, should the Luftwaffe appear. So I bumped the tail gunner of the lead ship and took his place.

It *was* pretty cramped. But I was able to swing the twin .50s, and the view was positively magnificent. Paris appeared far below in all its beauty, and I could make out famous landmarks such as the Seine, the Eiffel Tower, and Champs Élysées, and the Ile de la Cité. I wondered how the fun-loving Parisians were faring under the boot of *les Allemands*, and hoped we would soon set them free.

The sighting was done professionally, with the bombs from

our unit of twelve Forts disappearing into the roof of the larger structure, followed by a blasting explosion that split the roof of the hangar like a peeled orange. There was no flak except at the enemy coast, and no enemy fighters. A pure milk run.

Ike had moved his headquarters to Portsmouth on the southern coast of England, and my brother Thor was with him. He invited me down to spend a couple of days with him in his pyramidal tent. A good part of the Allies' great invasion force was quartered in that area under canvas with a netting of camouflage material covering the whole vast encampment.

I wangled a forty-eight-hour pass from Bob Williams and headed that way in the maroon Studebaker. It was no easy task to find the place, because everything about it was secret. However, Bob Montgomery managed to cut through reams of red tape and deposit me at Thor's tent.

Thor showed me around the great camp filled with tents as far as the eye could see, and even let me look inside Ike's trailer. But the Great Man was not in residence, and I didn't get to meet him again. In any event I don't suppose he would have remembered me from the short bash at Bassingbourn.

Always the best of friends, Thor and I were never more close. Our mutual admiration and respect were like bonds of blue steel. The invasion with its frightening risk, the prospect of thousands of casualties, even the outcome of the war itself, held us in thrall with the knowledge that our lives, if we had the good luck to survive, would never be the same.

I knew Germany was already defeated and, with a continued air offensive, would have eventually sued for peace. But the Allied invasion was such a monumental effort, involving almost immeasurable resources and millions of lives, that a defeat would have devastating political implications. We talked about this. "What if Eisenhower is thrown off the beaches with casualties in the hundreds of thousands?" I asked.

"A negotiated peace might follow," Thor speculated, "with an all-but-defeated Hitler winning Europe."

That night as we lay on our canvas cots, the buzz bombs came. Each one with its unmistakable motorcycle noise drew nearer and nearer to our camp and exploded somewhere outside the area. One flew directly over our tent, while we cowered in our blankets, as if they would protect us, but the deadly machine kept going until we no longer heard its buzz. The Jerries knew our camp was somewhere near Portsmouth, but either their intelligence was faulty or the buzz bombs weren't accurate enough to hit us.

Before leaving the area I looked up sister Jean's husband, Lt. James Kenneth Dobey. He was an enthusiastic glider trooper and eager to get into the fight.

16

D Day

Tom Beckett, my red-headed just-relieved Ops officer, burst into my six-by-six office in the Operations Block. He had completed twenty-nine missions and was happily anticipating his thirtieth, which would release him from duty with the Eighth and return him to the States. Lt. Col. George H. Koehne, one of the two combat-experienced majors from the Pacific Theater that Bob Williams had given me after the pounding we took at Oberpfaffenhofen, would take over Tom's duties in Operations. Tom was now showing George Koehne the ropes. Tom solemnly handed me a top-secret "twix" from Division. The date was June 5, 1944.

Usually he simply gave me a verbal report, if at all, of the next day's mission. I almost never bothered looking at the frag order that arrived by secure teletype (twix) in advance of the full Field Order. Tom's anomalous behavior rang an alarm bell.

My hand trembled a little as I held the yellow paper. I had a good idea what it contained: the long-anticipated invasion. It listed the targets we were to hit the next morning with maximum effort. These were enemy emplacements near the town of Caen in Normandy that the British forces were scheduled to take. I looked at the weather forecast on the large screen in the Ops Block. It predicted rain and clouds over the Channel and northern France. And it had been raining at Grafton for two days. I shook my head in frustration.

It looked as if we'd have to bomb on a PFF (radar pathfinder) ship. We had recently received better equipment for this that painted a radar picture of the ground. By dint of constant practice by lead bombardiers on an elaborate new simulator, which contained radar pictures of all the principal targets in Europe, our accuracy was improving. But only luck would cause us to hit a target as small as a gun battery. I prayed the French who remained in Caen would be deep in their bomb shelters when we appeared.

The twix also advised us to take precautions against a possible enemy commando attack on our base. If the Jerries had gotten wind of the invasion they might drop paratroopers to conduct sabotage. And most likely they would be dressed like American GIs.

I told Tom to call a meeting immediately of all senior staff officers, squadron commanders, and company commanders, and to have them assemble at the Senior Officers' Quarters. We had a lot to do.

The excitement was so palpable you could cut it with a bayonet as the officers filed into the large common room in my quarters. We had never before called a similar meeting there or one on such short notice and they, too, suspected what was up. But they sat in quiet anticipation.

"Gentlemen, tomorrow is D day." I paused. Unlike the behavior of the crews who greeted the announcement of a target with moans, whoops, whistles, and catcalls, these people were silent and intent. They were all mature leaders who were responsible for many others. "We're going to fly everything we have, perhaps two or three times over tomorrow, because the targets are so near. I know you'll all provide the same maximum effort that you have in the past. Just remember that there will be tens of thousands, perhaps hundreds of thousands, of GIs hitting the beaches tomorrow facing a deadly fire. We must help them all we can. We *must* not lose this one."

I turned the briefing over to thorough and taciturn Willie Buck. He seldom had much to say, but when he spoke it was well considered and factual. George Koehne indicated our targets and routes on a blown-up map of Normandy flashed on a screen. On his last mission Tom Beckett would lead the first flight of six to bomb gun installations near Meauvais. Bill Travis, Brig. Gen. Bob Travis's younger brother, would lead our major effort, a wing of twenty-eight to bomb two vital bridges southeast of the city of Caen. He'd fly in the PFF ship.

I wasn't about to be left out of this historical occasion and scheduled myself to lead one of the group formations in Bill Travis's wing. It irritated me that General Travis had denied me the honor of leading my own outfit, but there was no arguing with that arrogant general. Brother Bill was the executive officer of Bob's 41st Wing and there wasn't much I could do about the general's insistence that Bill lead.

Al Nuttall would lead the third effort of twelve to bomb some highway choke points near Caen. Ground exec Jim Taff would be in charge of the base defense plan. I was glad he had an active combat part to play. In the past, base defense had been something of a farce. We had the troops to do the job but they were all assigned to other duties. There had never been a significant enemy attack on bases of the Eighth Air Force except when one German long-range fighter followed home a flight of B-24s and shot down several while in the landing pattern. Sabotage was almost unheard of.

Fatherly "Pop" Dolan, our popular Intelligence chief who had flown in World War I, and master of ceremonies at most briefings, reviewed the latest Intelligence and cautioned all to carefully guard this secret until after the landings. Our station had been closed to all traffic, in or out, as well as any unofficial communications, just as soon as we got the twix. Times for formal crew briefings would be announced later in the usual manner.

I asked for questions. Taff noted that the gunpits were full of water. I replied that it was doubtful any major attack would occur, but to post his base defense people on the surface with as much cover as they could find. Remembering a lesson taught at the Military Academy, I noted that we should have some special identification and a password for our people that would keep us from firing at one another after dark.

"I want everyone to wear a white arm-band tonight on his upper left arm," I ordered. "A white handkerchief should do it. And I mean *everyone* from cook to colonel! Anyone without the arm-band can be judged a saboteur and should be arrested. Combat crews and all officers will wear sidearms. The password will be 'Keep the show on the road,'" our group motto, which proudly adorned our group insignia.

Bob Travis's brother, Bill, came over in the black Packard and attended our 3 A.M. briefing. I wished him luck as he left for the hardstand where the lead PFF Fort squatted. The weather was still overcast, but there was enough visibility for an easy takeoff. Twenty minutes after Tom's formation of six left the runway, Bill followed with twenty-eight, and twenty minutes after we had cleared, Nuttall's twelve started to leave the runway. Climbing up through the heavy clouds we found most of England socked in. But it was clear on top and we joined a gigantic parade of British and American bombers all headed for Normandy. I had never seen the grey sky so crowded with flying machines at various altitudes. How could Rommel survive this massive onslaught?

As we crossed the Channel the undercast thickened and there was nothing to see of Normandy. I was deeply disappointed for I had hoped to view the vast armada of ships converging on the beaches. There was almost no flak. And not a single enemy aircraft. Gen. Tooey Spaatz had told General

Eisenhower, "If you see any fighters they'll be ours." He was so right. We had absolute air superiority.

It was hard to imagine that the greatest invasion of all time was taking place below those clouds. We made our PFF run and dropped our bombs. Captain Crown reported that it was a good, clean bomb run and we should have hit our target. But we'd never know.

We turned right and flew the breadth of the Normandy coast, across the Cotentin Peninsula, to the island of Jersey, which stood out clearly on our radar, then north for a landfall near Weymouth, England, then headed for home. This wide loop was to keep us separated from the streams of other bombers coming in behind us.

Tom Beckett landed with his bombs five and a half hours after takeoff. He hadn't found his target; the cloud layer was too dense. Ground crews at Grafton hurriedly began to turn around Tom's Forts for another run to Normandy, and they did the same for the other returning Forts. Eager to do everything in their power to help the dramatic assault on Nazi Europe, they soon had all the Forts serviced and loaded with bombs. But no word came from Division to launch them. The Allied air forces, primarily fighters who could get below the overcast, had saturated the air over Normandy, and a fourth attack by the 384th wasn't needed.

Nuttall, too, had returned with his bombs. Neither he nor Beckett had radar bombing equipment and they couldn't locate their targets through the dense undercast. Late in the afternoon Division told us to scrub any further missions. So our full contribution that day was a force of twenty-eight Forts bombing by radar. It was a blue letdown.

For the rest of June we continued to put up anywhere from thirty-six to fifty-four Forts almost every day. The weather improved and we had some spectacular bombing results on airfields and marshaling yards. I led fifty-four to attack Dreux airfield on the thirteenth and we left it a smoking, cratered ruin, unusable for the Luftwaffe during the battle for France. No losses for us and only one abort caused by a malfunctioning airspeed indicator. This was my twentieth mission.

On the twenty-second I led a wing of forty to destroy the railway marshaling yards near Lille, France, with one of our groups attacking a buzz bomb site (code named Crossbow). We were flying thirty-six-plane wings but the spares we put up to fill in for aborts frequently decided to tag along and chalk up another mission even though there were no aborts. This accounted for the odd numbers of those Forts bombing, and indicated an aggressive, fighting spirit that pleased me.

On the last day of June I led the 41st Wing on a mission to bomb the airfield at Montdidier in France. Ten-tenths cloud cover over the target forced us again to bomb by radar. We saw no enemy aircraft and the flak was light. There were no aborts and no losses. Almost a practice mission.

17

Victory and Defeat

The massive Allied invasion forces had dug in on the Normandy beachhead, with forward units advancing inland fifteen miles. Starting June 17 a vicious storm raged for five days, destroying the artificial port fashioned with concrete barges called "Mulberries," and for a time the invasion was in danger of losing its vital supply line. For weeks it was slow going, until finally Gen. J. Lawton Collins's VII Corps charged up the Cotentin Peninsula and took the port of Cherbourg on the twenty-fifth, thus obviating our reliance on the Mulberries. After that there was no question that Eisenhower would soon be on the march to liberate France and advance into Germany.

My euphoria over the success of our troops in Normandy, and the fighting spirit my group was demonstrating, was marred by continued upsetting news from New York. Elise was still in the hospital at Mitchel Field. She had apparently recovered from the concussion caused by the automobile accident on the Queensboro Bridge. But on June 2, according to a letter from Alice Bucknam, Elise had had some female "repair work" done. She complained in letters about the almost unbearable pain, and I sent cables and flowers.

My growing concern for Kort and Voan, who had been without parents for over two months, dogged me. The several letters I received from family and friends assured me that the practical nurse taking care of them, Maude Wells Ehrhart, was doing more for the kids than Elise had done. This in itself was disturbing. Mrs. Ehrhart was even mending their clothes and buying new outfits for them. She was unquestionably a jewel, and had been the kids' foster parent since March 21. Before that, when Elise was in the hospital for an appendectomy, Mrs. Helen Bucknam and her daughter Alice had taken the kids into their home in Huntington. No doubt Kort and Voan were wondering whether either of their parents would ever return.

Elise wrote long letters about the need for Kort to have an eye operation that would cure his squint, and how the squint was getting worse and making Kort "nervous." Could she know so much about this while in the hospital? I suspected she had been talking to doctors there and possibly exaggerating Kort's problem. I also suspected that Elise's long absence from home— she'd been in the hospital over two months—was the primary cause of Kort's nervousness. Although Kort had shown an indication of this squint before I left New York, it had seemed to me that it was most evident when he was frightened or upset. Needless to say I questioned Elise's judgment, and wouldn't approve of such a delicate operation without first hearing from the eye doctors themselves. So her rambling letters didn't quiet my worries about the kids, no matter how efficient nurse Ehrhart seemed to be.

My mother had traveled to West Point to see my brother Drew graduate from the Academy early in June, and after that she had spent some time at our Jackson Heights apartment with Mrs. Ehrhart and the kids. She also visited Elise in the hospital and talked with the doctors there. No doubt she learned much from Mrs. Ehrhart about Elise's activities, but was advised by my "military friends" not to pass her information on to me. It would be too upsetting to me while I was engaged in combat, they told her.

Upon Mother's return to Reno, however, she gave Dad an earful, and he had no compunction about telling me. Dad wrote on June 13 about Elise's accident, "They arrived very late and very high at a cocktail party and were in bad shape when they left, and the accident resulted." But then he noted with some compassion, "The war has made a lot of people a little crazy." On June 28 he wrote: "I can't believe you have anything to gain by waiting before proceeding with a divorce."

I hadn't seriously contemplated a divorce. By now I knew that Elise had strayed and that Frank Fleet was her paramour. I began to realize that this was something more than just a casual wartime affair. Of course such tales of infidelity were as common as grass during the war, on both sides of the ocean; caused on the home front by loneliness, boredom, and the widespread relaxation of moral standards; and in the war zones it was a needed release from the iron grip of discipline, boring drill, and the constant fear of combat. My own hands weren't clean, and I couldn't blame Elise too much for succumbing to the widespread craziness. When this was all over, I thought, we could patch it up and live a normal life, at least for the sake of the kids.

To get an unbiased opinion, I asked the Red Cross to check on the kids and give me a report. Soon I was told that they were being well cared for by nurse Ehrhart, but that before she arrived in mid-March the kids had sometimes been left alone for days at a time, and were a concern to the neighbors. This I could not condone, and although I could bring myself to forgive Elise for her affair, I could not forgive her neglect of Kort and Voan.

My sister, Jean, who was living in Reno with my parents while her husband, Lt. Jim Dobey, served in England, offered to take Kort and Voan. So did Thor's wife, Mary, who had also moved to Reno with her three girls for the duration. When things got rough at home I had again urged Elise to move to Reno, where Mother, Dad, Jean, and Mary could help her with Kort and Voan, but she had flatly refused to do so. No doubt the pull of her affair with Frank Fleet influenced her decision.

I was greatly relieved when a friend wrote on June 19 that Elise had finally returned home after seventy-nine days in the hospital at Mitchel Field. Perhaps the affair with Frank Fleet would peter out now and she would show more concern for the kids. But on July 17 she wrote, "Yes, I'm nuts about or in love with Lt. Fleet. . . ." (He was not in the service, I learned, but an officer in the merchant marine.) And she ended the letter, "Take it easy but let me go free—you don't want me."

It was clear, from that last phrase, that I had caused her to feel rejected. The life of a service wife is hard at best, because the professional soldier must give his first loyalty to his country and the duties expected of him. He swears ultimate allegiance to the colors. Service wives may understand this, but few will accept it emotionally, because it is so contrary to common American values, where wife and children always come first. It took a very skillful and sensitive husband to keep a good wife under such circumstances, and I had failed the test. Now it was too late. The bond had been broken. And I was beginning to feel that divorce, with custody of the kids, was the only solution to the depressing situation at home. The whole mess was weighing me down as if I had lead in my veins.

Dad had consulted an attorney and wrote that a divorce was impossible without my being present in Reno, particularly if I wanted to gain custody of the kids. However, there seemed to be a way to get home. A regulation had come down from Eighth Air Force that permitted anyone who had flown twenty or more missions to go home on R and R (Rest and Recuperation leave) for one month and then return to the theater for another combat tour. I decided to ask Bob Williams for such a leave. I had never intended to give up my command at the end of a combat tour in any event. After asking experienced crews to volunteer for more missions than required, I certainly had to do the same. Bob quickly approved my request to return to the United States in August on an R and R.

Meanwhile the war stormed on. With a ground organization

designed to put up no more than eighteen Forts about twice a week, we continued to launch huge formations of thirty-six to forty-eight Forts into France almost every day. Each man on the ground was doing the work of three or more without complaint. In fact they seemed more than eager to do anything they could to contribute to the grand invasion.

We struck at airfields and enemy communications routes until the German army was all but stalled in place. General Spaatz fretted at our confinement to tactical targets and wanted to get back to the strategic effort, notably transportation and aircraft and petroleum production and storage. This latter was proving to be a true key resource, as Germany became more and more dependent on synthetic fuel. Moreover, our top air general wanted to get at the Luftwaffe fighters who had been sitting on the ground and building up their strength. He suspected that they would rise to defend their precious oil establishments, and he was right. So he got authority from Ike to attack strategic targets from time to time.

I led one of these missions on the sixteenth to bomb the Aero Engine factory seven miles south of Munich, not far from the ill-fated Oberpfaffenhofen where I'd taken such a beating in April. Although we encountered no enemy aircraft, the flak was even more pronounced. The 384th was a different outfit now than it had been on that April raid. It had become one of the most reliable and respected groups in the Eighth Air Force, and the crews knew it and were proud of it. There were no aborts, and all of our birds taking off bombed the target. Unfortunately one of our Forts was lost after "bombs away," presumably brought down by flak, although there was so much mist in the target area that no one saw the bomber leave the formation. We all hoped that it simply suffered nonlethal battle damage and headed for nearby Switzerland.

Clouds in the target area were banked high, and the scouting force of fighters that was about a half hour ahead of us radioed that we could get on top in the clear at 27,000 feet, which was about as high as we could fly with our big formation of heavily laden Forts. Fortunately we had plenty of time to climb in the clear before arriving at that mountainous cloud bank. But when we topped it, straining our engines to keep a good formation in the rarified air, we began to generate such dense condensation trails that those behind us were sometimes flying on instruments.

As we approached the target, accurate and heavy flak began to come up through the clouds, and many of our Forts, including mine, took battle damage. A large hunk of metal went through our fuselage just aft of the waist gunners, hitting nothing vital. I saw great orange explosions that must have come from very heavy-caliber guns, or perhaps rockets. Except for the missing B-17 piloted by Captain Coleman, all got back to England, although four had to land away from home at nearer airfields because of battle damage or wounded aboard.

We were puzzled by the absence of enemy aircraft on most of these raids—not that we wanted to see them. Why was Hermann Göring husbanding his Luftwaffe? Was it for defense of his petroleum resources? On June 20 we had hit a vast oil tank farm at Harburg, near Hamburg, and totally destroyed it, burning up great quantities of precious petroleum. This was probably one of the most telling blows against *der Reich*, although we didn't know it at the time. But canny Gen. Tooey Spaatz suspected it. Germany certainly couldn't fight without fuel for its tanks, trucks, and aircraft, and she was rapidly running out of gas.

On July 18 the 384th joined an Eighth Air Force raid on the V-2 weapon plant at Peenemünde. The V-2 was a far more threatening missile than the V-1 buzz bomb. It could be launched into the stratosphere and descend on a ballistic curve without warning, and it carried a larger warhead than the buzz bomb. Thanks to the superb bombing skill of Capt. Anthony

Palazzo, our strike that day did much to advance the CROSSBOW OPERATION and put the V-2s out of business. General Spaatz called it "The finest example of precision bombing I have ever seen." (This bombing of the advanced scientific facility at Peenemünde where the V-2s were designed and launched is best told by Lt. Col. Anthony Palaazo himself and is included as an appendix.)

In Normandy the enemy's clever use of the hedgerows near the town of Saint-Lô had stalled the Allied advance. The hedgerows surrounded the fields, and consisted of rock walls, ditches, and dense hedges and trees. They made ideal defensive positions. It was proposed by Gen. Omar Bradley to utilize our vast airpower to knock out the enemy emplacements protected in these hedgerows by hitting them with hundreds of thousands of bombs. The term "carpet bombing" best described this tactic, and the Eighth, along with the Ninth Tactical Air Force of two-engined medium bombers and P-51 and P-47 fighters, were to do the job.

The carpet-bombing operation was to take place on July 24, but the weather, which had caused Bradley to postpone the great COBRA breakout day after day, was still not good for bombing. Nevertheless most of the Eighth Air Force was airborne that day and never got the message to scrub the mission.

I led a thirty-six-plane wing to attack enemy strong points near La Chapelle en Jugar in the carpet area south of the Saint-Lô-Périers road. We dropped down to 13,000 feet to get under an overcast and approached the target area perpendicular to the road. This was risky business. If anyone dropped short, the bombs would strike our own troops north of the road, even though they had withdrawn 1,200 yards. Bradley had foreseen this danger and had recommended that the approach be made over enemy territory parallel to the front lines, but the air planners thought this would expose the bombers to too much accurate flak.

As we approached the drop zone I found it difficult, because of low broken clouds, to make out the road, even though it was supposed to be marked with red smoke. Some nervous bombardier in the group just ahead of me inadvertently dropped a couple of bombs. I saw them fall and knew what would happen next. Other bombardiers—we called them toggliers because none but the leader did any bomb aiming, while those following simply toggled off their bombs when they saw the bombs of the leader leave his bomb bay—would see the bombs drop and think they came from the lead bomber. Then they would toggle off their own bombs. The error would snowball until the whole group had dropped its bombs short of the road.

I grabbed my mike and yelled: "Don't bomb! Don't bomb! Don't bomb!" but it was no use. Bombs were dribbling from every bomb bay in the group ahead.

My bombardier was unable to see our primary target farther into the carpet-bombing area. Consequently we bombed a road junction that was visible. In my report to Division I complained about not having authority to make a second run, selecting a new IP (initial point to start a bomb run), because I thought if we had approached the target from a different direction we could have seen it, and I wasn't a bit happy with the perpendicular approach to the front lines.

The tragic consequences of the short drop by the group preceding mine—it was the work of the 379th Group, ironically perhaps the best of all the twenty-seven B-17 groups in the theater—were 25 friendly troops killed and 131 wounded.

Not having learned a lesson from bombing perpendicular to the road instead of parallel to it, the Eighth and Ninth Air Forces went back again on the twenty-fifth, and this time Bradley planned to attack in force on the ground and make the breakthrough. Although the weather was clear enough on the twenty-fifth to see the road, smoke and debris from the bombs dropped by leading groups obscured the road for those following. Again bombs were dribbled out early because of "bombsight trouble" and some forty-two medium and thirty-five heavy bombers dropped short. The tragic result of this second blunder was the death of 111 American troops, along with Lt. Gen. Lesley J. McNair.

One could argue that had the air attack been made parallel to the front over enemy-held ground at such a low altitude, more than ten aircraft would have been shot down and the total American losses would have exceeded the losses of our troops on the ground. Such are the heartbreaking decisions that senior commanders must make.

Yet the carpet-bombing tactic was successful beyond the most optimistic estimates. About twenty-five hundred bombers had dropped over five thousand tons of bombs on six square miles of terrain, churning it into a moonscape. Two German Panzer divisions were in the carpet area and their general later noted, "At least 70 percent of my troops were out of action—dead, wounded, crazed or numbed." Bradley then made the dramatic breakthrough that would soon develop into a German rout.

General Spaatz was determined to destroy the great synthetic oil works at Merseburg/Leuna. It was a tempting target, with its miles of pipes, cooling towers, and marshaling yards. We had bombed it in May, but it had been repaired and was now operating full blast. The 384th joined the bomber stream with thirty-six Forts three days after the carpet-bombing operation. We learned that the Merseburg area had become a hornet's nest of flak and fighters, and we were lucky to escape without a loss.

The next day we put up forty-six Forts for a second raid on Merseburg. Twelve of these would fly with the 41A wing, while I would lead the 41B wing of thirty-six, including two PFF planes from another group. This was the largest number the 384th had ever launched for a penetration into Germany, our one station providing four air groups. A shiver of pride surged through my body as I watched the forty-five silver Forts with triangle "Ps" on their tails wheel smartly into position. It was a far cry from the ragged flying of six months ago.

Thirty or forty ME-109s and FW-190s intercepted us in the target area and our gunners had a field day, claiming two destroyed and one probable. The enemy fighters didn't stick around; our escort of P-47s dove into them and they vanished, probably deciding to attack some less formidable formation.

Although we flew over ten-tenths cloud most of the way, the weather cleared and we were able to spot the great synthetic petroleum works when miles distant from it. The Jerries had attempted to hide it with smoke screens, but surface wind blew much of the smoke away.

The flak barrage above it was as thick as we had ever experienced over the Ruhr, which we called Happy Valley, and which up to now had been the most heavily defended area of Germany. Some crewman said, "The flak was so thick you could walk on it." Before entering the zone of flak my pilot pulled an ammunition can from under his seat and urinated in it. I had always been too scared to think about this, but suddenly it seemed like a good idea and I accepted the offered can. All we could do now was pray as the flak began to pepper our Fort with shell fragments and bounce us around like a boat in white water. We took many holes, but nothing slowed us down and none of our crew was wounded.

After "bombs away" we heard one Fort from our high group calling for fighter protection. No one had seen him leave the formation, and we didn't know where he was. That was the last we heard of him.

We had only one abort, caused by low oil pressure. Bombing results were excellent, and we didn't have to go back to Merseburg until mid-September. The great plant was put out of action entirely, and Hitler's Wehrmacht and Luftwaffe were almost immobilized as they screamed for fuel. We began to realize why so few enemy fighters were flying. The POINTBLANK campaign to destroy enemy aircraft production had been a failure because Germany had dispersed its factories and put some underground, but her thousands of new fighter aircraft sat on the ground with no one to fly them and no fuel to fill their tanks.

The Fifteenth Air Force based in Italy had again and again pounded the oil fields near Ploesti in Rumania. Armies and air forces drink petroleum products at prodigious rates, and this precious commodity for Hitler's war machine was rapidly running dry.

18

Rest and Recuperation

I left the 384th in the capable hands of Willie Buck and caught a C-54 ferry flight back across the North Atlantic to La Guardia Airport. When I arrived in New York I checked in at the Henry Hudson Hotel, where I had stayed during the formation of the AAF Antisubmarine Command. Jack Stack was the manager there and we had become good friends. He and his charming wife lent me their car and extended me many courtesies. I suspected that they knew a lot more about my problem than they let on.

I could hardly wait to see Kort and Voan, but my morbid thoughts about Elise had jelled into a deep anger and I had no intention of spending a single night with her at our Jackson Heights apartment. I called her the next morning and told her I was coming out to Jackson Heights. She must have learned earlier that I had returned. There was no sign of nurse Ehrhart or the kids. The apartment was spic and span, and Elise was as ravishing as ever in a neat housedress. The hungry thought rushed through my mind: were all the stories about her false? She had been such a good, loving mother and warm wife in the nine years of our marriage. Why had she changed so? Had she crossed me off completely after I went to England? Had she buried me before my time? Yet her early letters written the first month I was away had been long and affectionate. But why had she so neglected her children? Why? Why? Why? It just didn't make sense.

"Where are the kids?" I demanded.

"On the roof, playing in the sandbox there."

I rushed out and took the elevator to the roof. There they were, neat and clean, and enjoying themselves in the sandbox. My appearance was a complete surprise to them. Kort jumped up and I bent to wrap him in a hug. I saw no evidence of a squint. Neither eye was cocked out of focus. Voan grabbed me around the legs and I loosed one arm to enfold her. Their only words were "Daddy!" followed by little squeals. I couldn't hold back tears, not only for the joy of finding them hale and hearty but for the ache of what I was about to do to them.

Returning to the apartment with the kids I asked Elise to pack their clothes, that I was taking them to stay with Mildred Matthews, the wife of my friend Col. Frank Matthews, at Mitchel Field. Elise seemed resigned to this and made no objection. This attitude also puzzled me; why would she give up the children so easily?

I learned later that she had been evicted from the apartment at the end of July, four days before, and was not living there as it now appeared, but was staying with Fleet in a rented room nearby. The business at the apartment had all been a staged act, and she really had no place for Kort and Voan.

I arranged to meet Elise the next day at the apartment to help with the division of our personal effects and the moving. By then I had received a very damaging affidavit from Maude Ehrhart, prepared at the behest of Milton S. Lebe, a New York lawyer who had been retained through my father's efforts. I showed this to Elise and asked her to agree to a separation agreement, pending a Reno divorce, giving me custody of Kort and Voan. With this cold evidence put before her, together with her inability to cope with the children, she agreed without protest.

On August 8 I wrote Mother and Dad that "it's all sewn up. Tomorrow Elise will sign the settlement business and it will be a closed case. The car isn't fit to drive. I'll come by train. Ellen Mae [a teenage baby-sitter we had often employed] will come to look after the kids. I don't know enough about it, and can't risk anything happening to them. They are in good shape now—the only bright spot in this morass. Today has been worse than a mission over Germany. I talked with Elise and Fleet. . . ."

The separation agreement was formalized on August 10. It provided that Elise would get all household furniture, silverware, and other household effects, together with a cash settlement to be held by Mr. Lebe and sent to Elise in weekly installments to an address on Long Island, where Fleet's family lived.

Most important, of course, was that I would gain full custody of Kort and Voan, although Elise was granted visiting rights. She never took advantage of such rights. Later, in Reno, the ultimate divorce was a pro forma legal endorsement of the thoroughly prepared separation agreement by Mr. Lebe.

It would be a mistake to say that I survived this trauma with stoic equanimity. One night I drank heavily at the Henry Hudson bar and took the subway to Jackson Heights to look for Frank Fleet. This was before I had met him, and I had murder in my soul. I knew of a bar he and Elise had frequented, and I stormed in there asking for trouble. Fleet was not there, but had been. I canvased all the neighborhood bars but he managed to keep one bar ahead of me. I had no idea then where he and Elise were living, and I finally sobered up enough to give up the futile chase.

Later on it was necessary to communicate with Elise regarding the separation agreement, and I met Frank Fleet on one of these visits. He seemed to be a rather nice chap, quiet, unassuming, and somewhat apologetic. I was glad I hadn't found him on my drunken quest.

Frank and Elise soon married, and their union seemed

entirely successful. Obviously he could make her happy where I had failed. They raised two fine boys.

On arrival late at night in Reno with Kort, Voan, and Ellen Mae, I was met at the Southern Pacific Depot by Mother, Dad, my sister, Jean, and my sister-in-law, Mary. What an exciting and loving reunion that was! The women hugged and kissed me, telling me with their eyes how sorry they were that my home life had fallen apart. Dad, with a firm handshake and a look of pride, no doubt had thoughts of my participation in the war. Kort and Voan were bewildered by all the affection showered on them, and I soon introduced Ellen Mae, who was given a warm welcome.

We were all taken to 229 Maple Street, the white Victorian frame house where Mother and Dad had raised their family of four children. Long after Ellen Mae had tucked Kort and Voan into bed we sat at the large kitchen table and talked, and talked, and talked.

Dad was the state engineer of Nevada, and he managed a few days off so that we could all go to Carnelian Bay on Lake Tahoe where he and Mother owned a cabin called "Comus Cottage," with another in the rear called "Chipmunk Haul." With tents and cots the camp had accommodated as many as thirty people on one of their Comus Club outings. Now, with Mary's three girls, Dianne, Suzanne, and Marianne, present too, the camp was ringing with laughter, happy cries, and music from an ancient phonograph. Good smells of delicious cooking, combined with the pungent aroma of pine, brought back all the wonderful memories of summers spent at that well-loved hideaway, nestled in a grove of giant sugar pines, firs, and cedars.

And down below Comus, at the end of a pine-needle-covered path, rested the great Lake of the Skies, the magnificent turquoise-blue Lake Tahoe. Hardly had we arrived before young and old appeared in swimming suits. We rushed down to the boat dock and plunged into the icy-cold water, then sunned ourselves on the dock.

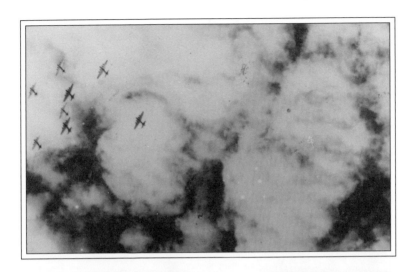

Top: *Photo taken from above, showing B-17s on bombing mission above layer of broken clouds.*

Bottom: *Dale Smith and B-17 crew back from bombing raid on Cologne. It was Smith's thirtieth mission.*

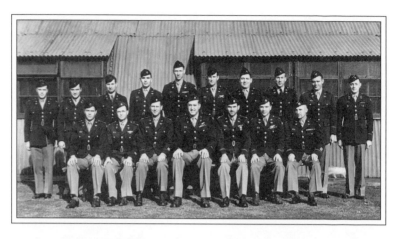

Top: *384th Bomb Group Headquarters officers, 1944.* Standing, left to right: *Harry W. Firstbrook; John M. Palmer; Carl R. Walker; John D. Herbert; Robert C. Chapin; Lyman A. Ragus; John E. Kreidler, Jr.; Charles A. Baker; John W. McKinnon; and Hobart W. Aiken.* Seated, left to right: *Nicolai Hansen; George H. Koehne, Jr.; Ralph W. Bond; Dale O. Smith; Henry H. Stroud; J. R. Wyatt.*

Bottom left: *Gen. Robert Travis, commanding general of the 41st Combat Bomb Wing, who never liked to finish second at anything.*

Bottom right: *B-17s of the 384th on bomb run. Note the flak bursting close to the lead plane.*

Top: *Flak from antiaircraft guns explodes in the sky nearby as B-17s fly over Nazi Germany. Note contrails from fighters higher up.*

Bottom: *Its tail shot off, a B-17 of the 384th goes down over Berlin, March 8, 1944.*

Top: *A flight of 384th Bomb Group B-17s high over Mannheim, in May 1944.*

Bottom: *Dale Smith* (center), *his brother Thor* (left), *and Jack Redding at Grafton Underwood before participating in practice bombing raid.*

Top: Screaming Eagle, *Dale Smith's own B-17.*

Bottom: *Aerial photo of Marienburg, Germany, after B-17 raid.*

Top: *Flak bursting near B-17s of 384th during mission over Germany.*

Bottom: *Back from a sight-seeing trip to Berlin.*

Top right: *Bombs away! A stick of bombs heads for Cologne, below.*

Bottom right: *Smoke billows from oil installations at Harburg after a successful bombing mission by the 384th.*

(SAV 32/565-)(20 6 44)(7221·12·25000)(Harburg)

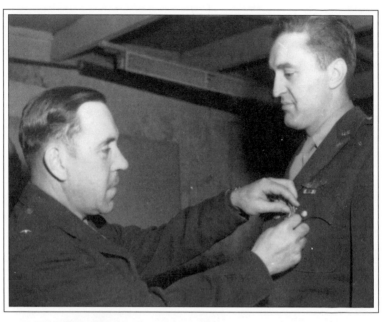

Top: *Brig. Gen. R. B. Williams, commanding general of the First Bomber Division, conferring the Distinguished Flying Cross on Dale Smith.*

Left: *Dale Smith turns over command of the 384th Bomb Group to Col. Ross Milton, November 1944.*

It shouldn't have been hard to forget the horrors of war in such an ambience, with love all around, or even to forget Elise—from time to time. Nevertheless, I felt a visceral depression that dampened my enthusiasm for almost everything, a constant ache in my gut that was caused by nothing physical. A sort of tidal change was taking place within me, and was flooding my goals with murky water.

Kort's squint began to manifest itself more often. The little guy missed his mother sorely, and I think he began to realize the finality of her absence. I took him to a renowned eye surgeon in Reno, who recommended an operation that would snip part of a muscle in the eye that was pulling it out of focus. After investigating, I became convinced that this Dr. Clark was as good a surgeon as I might find anywhere, and I agreed to the operation.

I had vivid memories of the terror I suffered as a boy of six when I was informed that I must undergo surgery a second time for the removal of tonsils and adenoids. Kort was seven and I didn't want him to suffer so. I decided not to inform him of the operation until the last minute. When they clamped a cone soaked in chloroform over my face, I had endured excruciating trauma, so I insisted on remaining with Kort during the anesthetic to assure myself that he wouldn't feel like he was suffocating, as I had felt. I was glad to learn that the art and science of anesthesia had progressed so far since that awful day in 1917 when I, too, had been incarcerated at St. Mary's Hospital.

As I helped Kort dress on the morning of the surgery I broke the bad news to him. My heart ached as his eyes opened in fear and the one bad eye cocked out. But he didn't whimper. I was proud of his courage. We walked hand in hand the three blocks to St. Mary's Hospital, and I stood by while the anesthesiologist carefully put Kort under without a struggle and Dr. Clark skillfully performed the operation. The prognosis was good, but in later years Kort had to wear glasses.

The month of "Rest and Recuperation" passed quickly—too quickly. I became much better acquainted with Kort and

Voan, who seemed to accept their new lives without complaint or even comment. I often wondered what they thought of their mother who had abandoned them, but we seldom mentioned her. I wanted them to have as fond memories of Elise as possible, and not to feel that they were any way at fault. They seemed to accept the fact that Elise had fallen in love with another man, and had chosen to live with him.

Ellen Mae had been sent back to New York shortly after our arrival in Reno, and sister Jean lovingly took over the rearing of Kort and Voan. It was a smooth transition, assisted by my mother and dad. I couldn't have asked for more support from my family, and on September 3 I started the trip back to England, with confidence that the kids would be well cared for.

I first wanted to see my brother, Drew, and thumbed my way in Army planes to Lockbourne Field, Ohio, where he was taking advanced pilot training. Drew was an eager second lieutenant now, ready to get in the war and win it single-handedly. I managed to con his commanding officer into letting him fly me from Lockbourne to Fort Dix, New Jersey, where I was to report for transportation to England.

We took off at dusk in an AT-6 trainer that had seen better days, and immediately ran into trouble. We couldn't seem to tune in a radio range with any accuracy and soon became confused as to our position. But we continued east into the night, while I fiddled with the radio receiver and eventually discovered that the tuning dial had slipped so that it registered about 10 kilocycles off. Once this was determined it was easy to make the interpolation and tune in the stations we needed. Drew, sitting and sweating in the backseat, looked upon this feat as a mark of sheer wizardry. I didn't disabuse him of this thought.

This minor glitch had frightened and tired me, however. The last thing I wanted to do was get Drew in trouble. Moreover, I had flown almost all night the night before. So I asked Drew to land at Omstead Field, Pennsylvania, before something else went wrong. There we could get a good night's rest at the visiting officers' quarters. The next day Drew flew me to Fort Dix and we said good-bye as he took off in the well-used AT-6 to return to Lockbourne.

Before the day was out I had completed all the necessary check-ins and paperwork and found a ride in a B-17G to Presque Isle, Maine, the jump-off place for flights to England. There I had to wait three days before getting a ride in a four-engined C-54 transport for the flight to Valley Airport in Wales, with an en route stop in Stephenville, Newfoundland.

The crew of the C-54 was a friendly bunch and the pilot let me do some of the flying. As we droned through the crystal-clear night of the North Atlantic and marveled at a magnificent display of the aurora borealis, my spirits rose. I was back in my element. My troubles were receding farther and farther. I was leaving them behind me. True, I was heading back to the terrors of war, but the dangers weren't as great as they had been when I had crossed this ocean last October. We were clearly winning the war now. It had become more of a mopping-up exercise, the coup de grace of Hitler's Reich.

I asked the radio operator if he could get through to Grafton Underwood and inform them that I was on the way. He not only did so, but received a reply that a 384th B-17 would meet me at Valley Airport and fly me home.

We landed at 0200 British Daylight Saving Time and taxied up next to the B-17. A burst of pride ran through me as a light shown on the big "P" inside a black triangle on its vertical stabilizer. How could they have responded so quickly to my message of a few hours earlier? It was my own ship, double naught seven, the *Screaming Eagle*. They must have had it sitting on alert.

As soon as our engines stopped and the door opened, a young major burst into the transport and ran up the aisle to shake my hand. It was the fearless Horace Frink, commander of the 547th Bomb Squadron, and one of my most loyal officers. I was overcome with emotion at such a warm welcome. Perhaps the 384th *had* missed me.

Hardly before I had thanked and said good-bye to the C-54 crew, Horace had had my B-4 and A-3 bags transferred to the B-17 and all that was necessary was for me to climb aboard myself. It was some difference from going through various checks and paperwork on the other side of the ocean every time I moved from one airfield to another. Horace let me fly as copilot. He had a complete clearance and knew exactly what route to take so that we wouldn't be fired on by British antiaircraft or intercepted by Spitfires.

It was my first and only night flight over England. There wasn't much to see. Blackouts were still in effect and no village showed a light. But as soon as we approached Grafton Underwood the runaway lights flared and Horace Frink greased our Fort in to a perfect landing. I thrilled at being back to the only home I knew. Here was a life I understood. Here there were no betrayals. Here we had a clear mission, and every one of us placed its importance above all else.

19

Reorganizing

The only regular Army Air Corps officer in the 384th besides myself was Willie Buck, a brave and conscientious professional, who had graduated from the Point in June of 1940. The only reserve officer with more service than Willie was George Koehne, who had been commissioned in August of 1939. It was Majors Koehne and Thacker who had driven home with me after a Division critique last spring, a welcome gift from Gen. Bob Williams. They were both highly competent and experienced officers and I considered myself very lucky to get them. Moreover, they had no feelings one way or another for the former C.O. of the 384th, Colonel Peaslee, and were completely loyal to me.

I couldn't put my finger on it, but I had lingering doubts as to the loyalty of some of the old-timers who had served under Peaslee. Their negative attitudes when I first joined still stuck in my craw, even though all of them had eventually swung into line and supported my hard-nosed discipline and many innovations. I knew I would feel much more confident when I had my own team in the key positions.

Back in December I had published a group circular that listed a number of goals for the group. At the top of the list, of course, was to rid the station of mud. Other goals included such items as a drained athletic field, a squash court, and even a basketball court. This grandiose "Grafton Plan" received considerable ridicule—after all, we were there to fly and fight, not try to live more comfortably, weren't we? Except for the basketball court, all the goals of the Grafton Plan had now been achieved and the troops were living much better. Following Napoléon's dictum that an army marches on its stomach, our messes were turning out palatable meals and the overall morale had improved remarkably. But I still hurt from the criticism and foot-dragging of last winter.

I wanted to find an appropriate spot for able George Koehne, whose seniority and experience qualified him for promotion to lieutenant colonel. To do this I established a new position for Tom Beckett—tactical inspector—and moved Koehne in as group Operations officer, S-3.

No one had more experience as an air leader than quiet Tom Beckett. Rather than planning missions and making out flight schedules, Tom could now concentrate on improving the actual flying of our group and bringing it up to the level of excellence I desired. Tom's acceptance of that aspect of my campaign had been somewhat less than enthusiastic. He had been one of Colonel Peaslee's favorites, and at one period had been the deputy group commander (air exec). Moreover, he had completed a combat tour and was getting FIGMO (Fuck you I've got my orders), the term used for someone who had received or was soon to receive orders for a move and was sluffing off his duties. He would soon be transferred Stateside.

Another major personnel change involved Willie Buck. He had never served under Peaslee. I suspected he had aspirations for a group command, but this opportunity hadn't materialized. From my point of view he was well qualified to command a group. During my absence on R and R he had led the 384th with much skill, although the month of August was a rather disheartening one because of the poor bombing weather. Willie had put up combat wings on seventeen days, mostly against tactical targets in advance of the rapidly moving ground armies. It had been a backbreaking effort, yet the group ran like a well-oiled machine. I imagine that the situation was changing so fast that the staff officers in Division Headquarters who advised General Williams on personnel matters had not recognized Willie's fine leadership.

Anyway, by September Willie had flown enough missions either to go home on R and R or be ordered to the States on a permanent change of station. I urged him to take the R and R, because I needed him, but he chose the latter course, and that left me with an opening for an air exec.

Bob Thacker, recently promoted to lieutenant colonel as a squadron commander, was the logical choice for that job. A forceful officer, Bob had served a combat tour in the Pacific before coming to me, and at Grafton he had demonstrated a superior brand of leadership both in the air and on the ground. With his cooperation and enthusiasm in the number two spot I was completely at ease. In my absences the group ran better under him than when I was present.

I made still another change, this time in the ground exec position. Division had requested an experienced nonrated officer to join the cadre in Russia that was preparing for the shuttle-bombing operations. I mentioned this to Jim Taff and he volunteered. Lt. Col. Ralph W. Bond was advanced to the ground exec position, and he served loyally, with full cooperation and initiative.

Thus by the end of September 1944 my three top assistants were men I had selected, and the shadow of the previous commander that had so haunted me had receded into legend.

This really was the high point of the 384th's fortunes. Our mission performance, as measured by the Eighth Air Force Operations Analysis Group, was right up on top of the twenty-seven B-17 groups in the theater. No matter how tough a mission had been, we flew squadrons in formation over the airfield on return, and a committee decided which squadron flew the tightest. Of course those Forts that fired red flares to indicate wounded aboard, or that were badly shot up, would be given clearance to land first. But the others would fly a parade formation. The winning squadron was announced at dinner time over the public address system that had speakers situated throughout the station. Our formations began to rival the best in England, and everyone took pride in this achievement.

One day a crippled B-17 staggered in from a mission and reported two engines out. I happened to be in the control tower and told the frightened pilot to land straight in, paying no attention to the wind "T," but he was so uptight he didn't respond. He came in low on the downwind leg and attempted a 180-degree turn to line up with the active runway, all the time dangerously losing altitude. My heart choked in my throat as I saw the bomber disappear behind the trees on the south side of the field. I was sure none of the crew could survive such a crash.

Jumping into a jeep I raced with the fire truck and ambulance across the field and into the woods. Coming to a fence, I saw the whole crew sitting on it. None was injured. I was overcome by this astonishing luck. Not far behind them lay the wreckage of their Fort. The left wing had hit the soft ground first and the underbrush and saplings had cushioned the fall. But the principal reason all had survived was that they had taken ditching positions with their backs against bulkheads and heads between their legs. I thanked God for the drilling we had done of this lifesaving exercise.

During the month I was away the complexion of the war had changed radically. After the spectacular breakthrough by Bradley following the carpet bombing near Saint-Lô, the commander of Wehrmacht forces in France, Field Marshal Gerd von Rundstedt, together with his subordinate, Field Marshal Erwin Rommel, commanding the Atlantic Wall, realistically assessed the disintegration of their defenses and so informed Hitler. The *Führer*'s response was to fire Rundstedt and replace him with Field Marshal Guenther von Kluge. But by the middle of July he, too, saw the hopelessness of their situation, and he and Rommel decided that when the time was ripe, German forces would retreat back to the German border, contrary to Hitler's orders to stand fast.

But on July 17 Rommel was seriously wounded by a strafing attack and left the theater. Three days later an unsuccessful attempt by Wehrmacht officers to assassinate Hitler caused chaos within the German high command. Rommel was suspected of being in on the plot and was forced to commit suicide. He was never replaced. Hitler lost confidence in Kluge and rightly suspected that he, too, was in on the assassination scheme.

With Hitler calling the shots from faraway East Prussia, Kluge was forced to deal with Bradley's breakout and sweep across France. Hitler refused to reinforce Kluge with the Panzer divisions in Calais until July 27, and then it was too late. Attacking to the east, Allied forces all but encircled the vast German army in the Falaise Pocket, killing ten thousand and capturing fifty thousand, although about that many escaped. By mid-August Allied forces from Italy landed in southern France and charged up the Rhône Valley to aid in chasing German forces to their Siegfried Line.

Eisenhower had hoped to bypass Paris, because its capture and occupation would consume too many troops and dwindling supplies. But Gen. Charles de Gaulle, and the commander of the French division, Maj. Gen. Jacques Leclerc, had other ideas, and defied Ike's orders by liberating Paris on August 25. Thor told me that Ike was livid at this insubordination, but could do nothing. The fall of Paris, combined with logistical problems, slowed Ike's advance and the German army escaped across the Seine River. At this point in the rout the Wehrmacht had suffered about a half million casualties and almost a quarter million captured. The Luftwaffe had lost over two thousand aircraft in the air and one thousand on the ground. Even so, with the apocalypse evident, Hitler fought madly on.

On September 3 Brussels fell to British forces, but the Allied armies were so short of supplies that they had to pause to regroup. This gave us a chance to continue our attack on synthetic oil plants. We went after the last one at Brüx in Czechoslovakia and hit it squarely. The Luftwaffe rose to defend this precious resource and shot down one of the 384th Forts.

After Antwerp fell General Eisenhower had a nearby port, but supplies failed to flow because the northern estuaries leading to the port were stubbornly held by the enemy. At the urging of Field Marshal Sir Bernard Montgomery, who commanded the northern army group, Ike planned a war-winning airborne attack on the low countries, with a swing south to encircle the Ruhr and take the enemy holding the Siegfried Line from the rear.

This ambitious effort, called Market-Garden, was a tragic failure. To begin with, our intelligence was faulty and the airborne army landed in a nest of German divisions that were, unknown to us, resting in the area near Nijmegen and Arnhem. Allied tanks, due to link up with the air drop, bogged down in the swamps lining the one road. But worst of all, bad weather hindered sending reinforcements and supplies by air, and severely restricted the ability of our air forces to bomb tactical targets.

My first mission after returning from the ZI was in indirect support of Market-Garden. On September 18 we led 41A combat wing, climbing up through a dense overcast to assemble at 15,000 feet. Our target was the marshaling yards at Hamm, the choke point for reinforcing enemy troops opposing the Market-Garden operation. Except for some moderate flak over the Rhine and at Hamm, we experienced almost no enemy opposition. One Fort, a spare that had flown with 41B, was hit by flak just after dropping its bombs on the target. When last seen it appeared to be under control.

Captain Crown at the bombing controls of the *Screaming Eagle* made a pretty good visual run on the target, but we flew over cirrus clouds immediately following "bombs away" and couldn't spot the hit.

During the next week we went after three more marshaling yards, with limited success because of the cloud cover. On September 27 I led the group on its two hundredth mission, an attack on the Cologne marshaling yards. Again the weather failed to cooperate and we bombed blind, with unobserved results. There was considerable flak over the target but we escaped unscathed by using a new tactic: combat wings were stacked at intervals of 2,000 feet in altitude, thus giving the flak gunners some difficulty in setting their fuses. By now, too, we were dispensing clouds of chaff, strips of foil giving a radar reflection that confused the gunners still further.

This Cologne mission was my thirtieth, and I led the Division of some five hundred Forts. (Eighth Air Force had credited me with three missions for my hundreds of hours of patrol while assigned to the Antisubmarine Command, so I actually had flown only twenty-five missions with the 384th and two with the 351st.) Anyway, I considered it some sort of a milestone, especially since it had occurred when the group had chalked up its two hundredth.

Division allowed us a stand-down and Grafton Underwood rang with merriment. Much planning had gone into this celebration. Formal invitations were sent far and wide:

The Commanding Officer and Officers and Enlisted Men of
The Three Hundred and Eighty Fourth Bombardment Group
U.S.A.A.F.
Request Your Company at
Their Two Hundredth Mission Celebration

A separate sheet listed the program:

"Awards Banquet"—Officers Mess Hall—1800 hrs.
Guest Speaker: Brig. Gen. Robt. F. Travis.
D-A-N-C-I-N-G

All Enlisted Men   Hangar #1   2030 Hrs.
(Music by George Elrick & his BBC Orchestra)
(and Entertainment)

—Buffet and Four Huge Bars—

Officers   Officers Club   2030 hrs.
(Music by "Flying Yanks" Orchestra)

Zebra Club Members   Zebra Club   2030 hrs.
(Music by Stratton-Audley G.I. Band)

Transportation for guests will be provided from:

Northampton	Market Square	1900 till 1930.
Kettering	George Hotel	1900 till 2000.
Woodford	Cycle Shop	1915 till 1930.
Corby	Raven Hall	1930 till 2000.
Brigstock	ATS camp	1945
Brigstock	Three Cocks Inn	1945 till 2000.
Brigstock	WLA Hostel	1945
Lilford Hall	Nurses Quarters	1930
Newport Pagnell	WRNS Quarters	1915
Finedon		1915 till 1945.
Geddington	Star Inn	1930 till 1945.

****

All Guests Will Be Delivered to Hangar No. 1 First!
All Personnel are Urged to Invite Their Own Guests

****

Bring your canteen cups to the Dance in Hangar #1

Sunday

Novelty Events: Administrative Site—1500 hrs.

"Sack Race"—(For Men Only).

"Three-legged Race"

"Relay Race"

"Piggy-back Race"

"Wheelbarrow Race"

"Slow Bike Race"

Bicycle Derby—Around perimeter track—1600 hrs.

Baseball Game—Station 106 vs. 8th AF All Stars

****

Scotch Bagpipe Band 7 Highland Dancers—Admin. Site 1930

hrs.

****

U-S-O Stage Show   Station Theater   1800 and 1930 hrs.

Including:

Artie Conray . . . . .MC & Comedian

Drohan & Dupres . . . .Comedy Act

Vivian Moore . . . . .Dancer

Fearne Downes . . . . . .Accordionist

****

"KEEP THE SHOW ON THE ROAD"

Needless to say our fleet of trucks was kept busy and girls were plentiful. Trucks left the station at midnight to return the girls to their towns, but there were never as many passengers returning as arriving. I turned a blind eye to all this hanky-panky. Concupiscent young men who were putting their lives on the line almost every day needed to blow off steam and relax.

Not long after this celebration, Bob Williams called to say that he was sending me a copy of a letter from the Pentagon and wanted to know my reaction. The letter read:

28 Sep 1944

Major General Robert B. Williams
Headquarters 1st Bombardment Division
APO 557
New York, New York

Dear Bob:

Thanks for your answer to my letter requesting Colonel Dale Smith. While I appreciate your cooperative attitude and your offer of Colonel Robinson or Colonel Reid in lieu of Smith, I am afraid that the substitution is impossible inasmuch as both of these officers are already earmarked for other assignments.

I have not made an official request for Smith until I could write to you again and see how you feel about the matter knowing that neither Robinson nor Reid are available to me. Although I feel that Smith is particularly qualified for assignment as Deputy Chief of my Requirements Division, it is not my intent to embarrass you with an official request if you do not prefer to release him. I hope that since last writing, events may have transpired which will permit you to see your way clear to releasing Smith. Please let me know how you feel about this.

With best wishes, I am

Yours sincerely,

H. A. Craig,
Major General, U.S.A.

Upon reading this letter I called Bob immediately and told him I had no interest in leaving the 384th for a Pentagon assignment, even though this proffered spot might mean general's stars. He was guarded in his response, but told me he hated to turn down General Craig a second time, and that he'd let me know what he intended to do.

I had made a pact with myself and the group that I would either finish out the war with the 384th or die in the attempt. Now, with this new development, my resolve was shaken, and I needed to talk it over with someone. Bill Gross, of course.

"What you need, Stooge," Bill advised (I had been the "stooge" ever since he won his stars), "is a trip to Paris. The Eighth has been sending some group commanders over there and a lot of staff officers to examine the bomb damage. I think it's time you and I go, too. You dropped bombs on Orly Airport once, didn't you?"

"Yeah, and I *saw* the bomb damage from the tail gunner's seat."

"Never mind that. There's plenty of other targets we ought to examine. Leave it to me. I'll set it up for both of us." Bill made decisions fast, even before I could answer.

We flew over in a Gooney Bird (C-47) and were billeted in the bridal suite of the Ritz Hotel on the Place Vendôme. It looked like luxury, until we discovered that there was no heat in the building and the restaurant served starvation meals. But Paris was alive and bubbling with a mass euphoria over its newfound freedom, and everyone treated us like conquering heroes.

Bill had learned that coffee was as scarce as gold in Paris, and so we arrived with our musette bags stuffed with small cans of Nescafé. One of these tins of instant coffee, presented to a bellboy, would produce a bottle of champagne. To combat the morning cold, Bill and I lay in our linen sheets and drank champagne for breakfast.

At the Ritz Bar I ran into a young second lieutenant, Bill Elsworth, from San Antonio. Back in flying school days I had dated his sister. He had arrived in Paris with a logistics team a few days after the city had been liberated. He invited us to a party being given by some friends of his. Bill and I readily accepted and the second lieutenant led us out to the curb where a huge black German limo was parked. "That's mine," the young second looey boasted. "I liberated it from a German general."

Before getting into the big car the young host led us to the front where a cover hid the license tag that usually displayed the stars of a general officer. Ceremoniously he removed the cover and there on the tag was the gold bar of a second lieutenant.

Then our friend drove around Paris, stopping here and there to pick up *jeunes filles*, each one piling into the back of the giant limo with bottles of champagne until the floor of the backseat was paved in bottles. The one commodity that the Parisians had successfully hidden from the occupying Germans was champagne.

Next day a gentleman we had met at the party took us to the steeplechase races at Auteuil racetrack in the Bois de Boulogne. Paris was on a perpetual binge, and on this sunny day the stands were crowded with laughing people. Our new friend took us to a watering hole under the stands, where great tubs sat filled with ice and wine bottles. Beautiful French women, dressed in high fashion, seemed to be everywhere. We were amazed at this lavish display; it was difficult to imagine that these people had so recently been subjected to the German boot.

Between races our new friend would take us to the exercise paddock to look over the horses for the next race. He would tell us which horses to bet on, but we were skeptical and for a few races made our own judgments, and lost, while our friend's horses always finished in the money. Soon we began to take his uncanny advice and won handsomely. That evening we invited our friend and everyone else we knew in Paris to dinner at the Ritz. The famous old hotel did pretty well for us, and we managed to spend our winnings.

For two days, except for our examinations of bomb ruins, the war was far from our thoughts, and Bill and I had met a people who were determined to enjoy life. Yet not far away the war still raged, and we had to return to our grim duties. The respite had not helped me to make a decision about my possible reassignment. Perhaps the decision was being made for me.

20
FIGMO

It was not long after we returned home from that trip to Paris that Gen. Bob Williams invited me to dinner at his comfortable quarters near Bramton Grange. I suspected he had something confidential to tell me, and I was correct. "Dale," he said, pinning me with his ferocious working eye while the glass one was cocked somewhere to the south, "I've decided to make you available to General Craig. Hap Arnold's new policy is to staff AAF Headquarters, as far as possible, with officers who have seen combat, and this policy was revealed to me in no uncertain terms. So I have to go along with it."

Getting policy from Gen. Hap Arnold, who commanded the U.S. Army Air Forces, was like words from a burning bush. He was soon to be the only five-star general in the AAF, and he commanded great air forces all over the world. By the end of the year he had the awesome number of 72,700 aircraft at his disposal, crewed and supported by 2,350,000 personnel.

I turned up my palms in resignation. It wasn't too much of a surprise. After clearing his throat Bob told me that I'd soon be getting orders, probably in a couple of weeks. He cleared his throat again and said he was sending Col. Ross Milton to the 384th as my replacement. Ross was Bill Gross's deputy and one of the best combat leaders in the Eighth. This was good news, because I knew he'd be a great leader and keep the 384th on top.

I told Bob that I was delighted with his selection, that I considered Ross long overdue for command of a group, and that in my estimation there was no better combat officer in all of England. "The 384th will be in good hands," I said.

Bob expressed his gratitude for my willingness to accept the reassignment without putting up a fight, which I might have done had he selected anyone but Ross Milton to replace me. I had a very proprietary feeling about the 384th. It was *my* group, and had been dragged out of the doldrums by dint of much sweat and heartache. I was inordinately proud of it and the fine men that made it. Now, like a knight in shining armor, the group sparkled with the best, an example of one of the finest B-17 outfits the United States could produce.

Bob noted that the 384th had become one of his best groups; he was aware of my attachment to it, but he couldn't appreciate how deeply that attachment had become. Losing it now was a wrench almost akin to losing Elise.

I looked into my drink as if to find some appropriate words there. "Of course I'm flattered that someone in the Pentagon wants me," I said, "and I know you wouldn't want to buck Hap Arnold's policy." I wondered whether Arnold remembered me. He had commanded the 1st Wing at March Field when I was assigned as a second lieutenant to the 7th Group at Hamilton, one of his groups. I had met him a number of times, very briefly, but that was a long time ago.

"I wonder how General Craig got my name," I said, "I hardly know him. But I've taken the Queen's Shilling, and of course I'll go wherever she tells me to."

"Good, that's settled then," Bob said with some relief. "Let's have another drink."

I managed, perhaps awkwardly, to tell Bob that he was the best boss I'd ever had, or probably ever would have, and how I hated to leave his command, remembering how he backed me up against all the powers in London during that mud crisis.

He thanked me with some embarrassment. "But don't

forget Bob Travis," Bob added. "He's done more for you than you realize."

I only nodded my head as another scotch and water was thrust into my hand by Bob's orderly.

Horace Frink was scheduled to lead a wing against the marshaling yards at Münster and his Fort was out of commission. I lent him *Screaming Eagle* and cautioned him to take good care of her. Again, the Jerries didn't cooperate. It was a punishing raid and *Screaming Eagle* was badly shot up. We got word that Frink landed at Brussels. The leader of the low group, Maj. Thomas Hutchinson, was missing, but later turned up in France. I was glad that Frink could get into Brussels and that he and his crew were unharmed. He called me on the phone from there. I was amazed at how quickly our communications people had established such services.

"I lost two engines," he said, "but I think with a little skillful maintenance one, number three, can be repaired. Number four has had it."

"Think you can fly it out on three engines?"

"Yes, Sir. If we strip it of all unnecessary weight, like the number four engine and the ball turret."

"Sit tight," I said. "I'll fly over there tomorrow with some good mechanics and the parts." Horace then listed all the parts his engineer believed would put the right inboard engine into commission.

Bob Williams approved of this sentimental journey to save *Screaming Eagle* from the scrap heap. On landing at the Brussels municipal airport the next day I found the field littered with shot-up aircraft of every description, both Allied and German. The airport was a Sargasso Sea of dead warplanes. The only cleared-off place was the runway on which we landed. It was lined with battered derelicts.

Horace met me in a jeep he had scrounged from the Canadians who occupied the city. Like Paris, Brussels was on a perpetual binge, with happy crowds milling through the streets, bars, and stores. We Yanks were a sensation, since the Belgians had seen nothing but German and British troops. Horace had taken good advantage of this friendliness and introduced me to a charming family, who attempted to show us all of Brussels. They even invited us to their home, where precious champagne was dug up from a wartime hiding place.

Our mechanics had *Screaming Eagle* ready to go in a couple of days. Since it was still his mission, I let Horace fly while I took the copilot's seat on the right. He turned the three-engined Fort around at the very end of the runway, expecting the crippled bird would require every foot to get airborne.

When Horace released the brakes with the three engines roaring at maximum RPM and manifold pressure, the ship immediately began to slew to the right, toward where the dead outboard engine once was. Although we had cranked in full left rudder on the trim tabs we now both had to strain our legs with all our might to depress the left rudder pedals and keep the big ship on the runway for a few hundred feet until speed picked up. Then, even though Horace throttled back some on the left outboard engine, the big ship again began to slew right toward the line of shot-up craft lining the runway. I began to think this takeoff on three engines wasn't such a hot idea and visualized us slamming into the derelicts. Just when it seemed a crash was inevitable *Screaming Eagle* broke ground and lifted off the runway, soaring over the wreckage with what seemed only inches to spare. As soon as we settled down to level flight Horace and I stared at each other and shook our heads in disbelief. Once again we had been blessed with astonishing luck. We flew home at 1,000 feet so that Allied antiaircraft could clearly recognize us as friendly.

Screaming Eagle wasn't long for this world, however. Our maintenance people patched her up like new and I flew her on one more mission. It was to that nemesis of the Eighth Air Force, Schweinfurt. A year earlier we had suffered two bruising battles in the effort to destroy the enemy's ball bearing industry, and during the ensuing year we had gone back again and again, but intelligence informed us that the Germans had miraculously repaired some of their plants and were still turning out the precious round steel balls needed to build tanks, trucks, and aircraft.

When we had attacked the Schweinfurt plants in 1943 we had been met by swarms of aggressive enemy fighters and a sky black with accurate exploding flak. No more. On this raid of October 9, 1944, the Luftwaffe, what was left of it, didn't rise to oppose us. Our Little Friends had nothing in the air to challenge them, and most went down on the deck to shoot up whatever military target they could find.

We had to release our bombs on a drop by a radar ship, because the target was obscured by a solid undercast of fleecy clouds. Moderate flak came up through the clouds but was generally inaccurate. Even the enemy flak gunners were losing their fighting spirit—or perhaps they had given up attempting to defend the ball bearing plant. We returned to Grafton Underwood with no losses and little battle damage. It was my last mission.

Ross Milton had reported to Grafton Underwood and quickly demonstrated his ability to lead the group. There seemed to be no reason why I should hang around awaiting orders. Even a commander can get FIGMO, and with two full colonels in the headquarters the group was in a state of indecision.

Periodically we held award banquets where it was my pleasant duty to hang Air Medals, Distinguished Flying Crosses, Purple Hearts, and sometimes Silver Stars on the chests of deserving heroes. On October 20 we held such a ceremony and I made my farewell speech. I told them why I was leaving the 384th and expressed my regret because

> commanding this group is the best job in the Air Force . . . the 384th is undoubtedly the best group in the AAF, and this command has been the greatest adventure of my life. So many vivid experiences . . . fine, noble airmen and ground crews . . . wonderful memories of brave men . . . guts here is a common thing . . . the daring . . . the sacrifices . . . the sad losses of good friends and great fighters . . . but you carried on to victory, individually and collectively. . . . I hold the 384th as the dearest thing in my heart. . . . You are fortunate in having Colonel Ross Milton as your new commander. . . . He will lead you to new triumphs. . . . Thank you for giving me this memorable opportunity and for your willing support. . . . Good luck and good bombing!

My orders hadn't arrived yet, but informally I turned over the command of the group to Ross and headed for London and the headquarters of the United States Strategic Air Forces in Europe (USSTAF) to find out what was what. The personnel people there advised me to be patient, that orders were on the way; in the meantime why didn't I get briefed by the planners to see what the postwar situation would be like? This information would probably be of help to me when I got to the Pentagon (and perhaps I could influence the Pentagon with some USSTAF thinking).

It interested me that the planners were devoting most of their time to the problem of occupying Germany after its defeat. Obviously, they, too, considered the war won and believed that Hitler would soon throw in the towel. But they didn't visualize the rapid advance of the Soviet war machine, which would split Germany in half and cause innumerable occupation problems.

Moreover, they didn't foresee that Hitler had such a diabolical hold on the German army that he could throw one last dying punch in the Ardennes and penetrate our lines in the Battle of the Bulge. But that all happened after I was comfortably ensconced behind a desk in the Pentagon.

Thor was in Paris, herding the legion of war correspondents following the Allied armies. Many of them, along with Thor, were living in the Hotel Scribe. I wanted to have one last visit with Thor, and after I had digested all the planning stuff I could understand, I inquired if I might go to Paris while awaiting my orders to the ZI. No objection whatever, said dour Gen. Tooey Spaatz, America's top airman in the European Theater. In fact he asked me to get briefed by Ike's staff and learn what I could from his planners about what they considered postwar Europe would look like, then to drop by on my return and let him know what I had learned.

Perhaps I was asking too many embarrassing questions at USSTAF, such as why we didn't bomb flak emplacements where the guns were still taking a toll of our bombers. Such targets would be more productive than bombing burnt-out ball bearing factories; what was left of them could hardly make any significant contribution to the German war effort at this late date. Getting rid of flak guns would also help the ground forces, because the Jerries could lower their .88s for use in the ground battles.

And why didn't we bomb their radar sites? They would be easy to find with an electronic homing device. Radar was directing all the punishing flak we got when flying above the clouds, not to mention keeping track of the routes and strengths of our attacking formations.

And couldn't we give the air commanders a little more authority to use their discretion when leading missions? I'd flown by juicy targets such as Luftwaffe airfields that were in the clear, to bomb inaccurately on instruments the cloud-covered target we'd been ordered to attack. Although greatly improved over the earlier methods of blind bombing, the current H2X bombing radars were still not up to the accuracy of visual bombing. Why not let the man on the spot make the decision on which targets to hit? Couldn't he be briefed in more detail on the priorities and strategy involved? Why did he have to be launched like a guided missile or an artillery shell? Why not let the man on the spot carry on a real air battle?

And couldn't we send the B-24s to the Pacific Theater, where their low-altitude range would be more useful, and fill up those B-24 groups with the new B-17Gs that were coming to England in swarms? The B-17Gs were far better and safer than the B-24s for the kind of flying we were doing in Europe. I had had extensive experience with both aircraft.

Although they thanked me for my suggestions, I think the brass there were glad to get rid of me. A good staff usually seeks advice from the field, but also hates to have its preconceived ideas disturbed. Since we had more new B-17Gs at Grafton Underwood than we had crews to fly them, and no transports, the general agreed to my taking *Screaming Eagle* to Paris. Ross had been in the theater longer than I, and had suffered through some of the roughest raids. He needed a holiday and I gained authority to take him along as copilot.

Returning to Grafton Underwood I presented this enticing invitation to Ross, who was more than happy to accept. The weather didn't look too good over France the next day but there was some ceiling over Paris, maybe 500 to 1,000 feet, and we were cocky enough to believe that with no one shooting at us and with no bombs in the bomb bay, we could sneak into Tousous le Noble airfield with complete safety. Having survived so many dangerous combat missions, we had forgotten how inherently dangerous an airplane could be, even when no one was shooting at it.

The weather wasn't bad at Grafton and we took off with

light hearts for Gay Paris. *Screaming Eagle* had never flown better, its engines singing a happy song of delights to come. But as we crossed the Channel the ceiling began to lower and we were just under the overcast at 1,000 feet. No matter. Plenty of ceiling for a comfortable flight. Oh, oh. Soon we had to drop down to 500 feet to stay underneath the scud. Still okay for a couple of veteran combat pilots like us. As we approached Paris we were forced still lower, to 300 feet, while flying in and out of wispy fog banks. It grew dark. It would have been the better part of valor then and there to have made a 180-degree turn and headed back to England. But no, the vision of a holiday in Paris was too enticing. We charged ahead.

A radio beacon helped us to find Tousous le Noble airfield and by that time we were skimming the tops of buildings at about 200 feet. A light rain was coating our windshield, and visibility was down to maybe two or three miles.

The airfield had been heavily bombed, all right. The "Notices to Airmen," which we had failed to read, reported that the bomb craters had been filled in but the fill might be soft, and we should avoid them on landing. Visitors were cautioned to land between mattress covers that had been staked out to indicate a recommended landing strip without filled-in bomb craters. But this information wouldn't have done me much good anyway, because with the poor visibility I saw no mattress covers.

So I banked *Screaming Eagle* around the airfield like a fighter pilot coming home after five victories, with the right wing in the clouds, and leveled off on the final approach toward what looked like a solid landing area. I called for full flaps. We were coming in too fast, and Ross yelled, "Go around! Go around!" A building appeared dead ahead at what would be the end of our roll, but I was sure I could stop before that, and I wasn't about to go around again with my left wing almost scraping the ground. I hadn't been able to raise the tower on the radio, but just then a green flare shot up from it. All was in order.

We touched down comfortably in the soft earth and thought we were home free. Then, WHOMP, the landing gear rolled through one of those recently filled-in bomb craters. It was a fearful bump, and I wondered if our undercarriage had been damaged. Marveling once more at the ruggedness of the B-17 we continued to roll, losing speed, and I breathed easier. Then again, *WHOOMP*, as *Screaming Eagle* shuddered in and out of another mud-filled crater. Finally, just as our landing roll was about to end, our cruelly punished Fort slid down a steep incline into a really deep mud hole. Its wheels disappeared, completely buried in the largest bomb crater of all. Our wings and fuselage rested on the ground, our engines had abruptly stopped as the props dug up earth, and the undercarriage, deep in the mire, was nowhere to be seen.

Screaming Eagle was a sorry sight. After walking around it I bent over and asked Ross to kick me. He did.

Needless to say I was royally pissed off with the engineers who had filled in these bomb craters with loose earth and mud instead of crushed rock. The idiots would have done better to leave the craters exposed, and I was still further annoyed that the tower had fired a green flare and no operator had warned us that our approach was wrong. I supposed all the personnel responsible for this airfield were drinking wine on the Champs Élysées. Moreover—and this was the crowning insult—I was later informed by the engineers that they could not extract *Screaming Eagle* from the mudhole.

So there rested that great warplane, and I suppose parts of it are still there. Perhaps it was more fitting for *Screaming Eagle* to be buried there in France than for it to rot in an Arizona desert boneyard where thousands of her sisters were soon to end their service. Every time I land in Paris I wonder if that muddy field has grown into a modern international airport, and if I'm landing over the rusted earthly remains of *Screaming Eagle*. Perhaps some millennia hence an archaeologist will dig up portions of it

and try to reconstruct the form that was once the pride of my
flying days. Rest in peace, old friend. You protected me again
and again and always brought me home safely.

The demise of *Screaming Eagle* didn't dampen our enthusiasm for Paris. Thor and I greeted each other warmly. He had
been there long enough to know his way around pretty well, and
he made arrangements for my briefing by some of Ike's planners.

Being somewhat closer to the battle than Tooey's USSTAF,
Ike's SHAEF (Supreme Headquarters Allied Expeditionary
Forces) planners seemed a little more practical. Their immediate concern was crossing the Rhine, encircling the Ruhr, crush-
ing the last resistance of the Wehrmacht, and advancing to make
contact with the Russians without shooting at each other. I got
the impression then that Ike didn't plan to take Berlin. Like
generations of other West Pointers he had been imbued with the
doctrine that the enemy forces in the field should be defeated
first, and that no general should waste his resources by occupying the enemy capital before then. The example of Napoléon's
defeat after occupying Moscow was a vivid lesson we all had
studied.

Perhaps in this instance the doctrine didn't apply. It was
Churchill's view that Allied forces should beat the Russians to
Berlin, but the damage had already been done when the Allied
powers had agreed to carve up occupied Germany so that Berlin
rested within the Russian sector. Ike didn't see any sense in
wasting American lives to take territory that later would have to
be turned over to the Russians. In the euphoria of imminent
victory and Allied cooperation, no one foresaw the problems
that would be caused by postwar Berlin.

One rainy night Thor and I found a taxi that burnt wood in
some ugly contraption on its roof, and we were taken to a wild

nightclub in the Montmartre. The only transportation we could find when we started back to the Scribe Hotel was a horse-drawn cab. We listened to the clop-clop-clop of the nag's hoofs on the wet pavement as we slowly made our way home in the rain, and we talked of all the great dreams we had for our postwar lives.

Thor had been overseas for almost three years, and wouldn't be returning for another year. He envied my return after little more than one year in England. Always where the action was, Thor was to cross the Remagen Bridge over the Rhine when it was seized, be among the first troops to make contact with the Russians on the Elbe River, and witness the German surrender at Reims on May 7, 1945.

Ross and I returned ignominiously to Grafton in a C-47 Gooney Bird and we tried to avoid questions about what had happened to *Screaming Eagle*. My orders to AAF Headquarters had arrived, and the officers at Grafton Underwood were planning a farewell party. They had invited all of my friends in England and many had accepted. It was a bash long to be remembered, or perhaps better forgotten.

They sent a B-17 down to my brother-in-law's station and fetched Jim Dobey. His glider outfit was preparing for a Rhine River crossing and vertical envelopment. Bill Gross came, of course, while Bob Travis and Bob Williams stayed for dinner but not for the heavy drinking afterwards in the Officers' Club. Someone pounded the piano while we sang bawdy wartime ballads off-key and at the top of our lungs. Bill's favorite was "Roll Your Leg Over."

It went like this:

> I wish all the girls were like fish in the river,
> If I were a beaver I'd tickle their liver.
> Oh roll your leg over, oh roll your leg over,
> Oh roll your leg over th' man in th' moon.

I wish all the girls were like little white rabbits
If I were a hare I would teach them bad habits.
(Chorus)

I wish all the girls were like Hedy Lamarr
I'd try twice as hard and I'd get twice as far.
(Chorus)

There was a pause after each verse while someone would come up with a new wish that rhymed. And, of course, there were lusty verses of "Bless 'Em All":

There were Fortresses over Calais
Bound for Old Limey shores
Covered all over with petrified men
All scared and flat on the floor.

Many a Heinkle has pumped us with lead,
Many a Messerschmidt too.
They shot our hydraulics
They shot off our ballics
So cheer up my lads, bless 'em all.

(Chorus)
Bless 'em all, bless 'em all
The long and the short and the tall.
Bless all the sergeants and W.O. ones,
Bless all the corporals and their bastard sons.
For we're saying good-bye to them all,
As into our Fortress we crawl.
There'll be no promotion,
This side of the ocean,
So cheer up my lads bless 'em all.

There were several verses to this popular ballad, one of which would always be addressed to the highest-ranking person in the crowd:

In ten thousand years
When they're digging for peat
Some bloody place in Wick,
They'll find a Fortress
All covered with peat
And old Bill Gross at the stick.

Toward the end of the evening, as the crowd began to thin, Bill and I found ourselves sitting at the bar downing the strong drinks that we hardly needed, served by Primo, our ubiquitous bartender, and exchanging insults.

Bill was the "maestro" in the game of one-upmanship we had been playing for years, and I the "stooge." This was not just because Bill had won the stars of a brigadier general, but because one evening when I was visiting him at Bassingbourn he had served me four delicious fried eggs, sunny-side up. An unheard-of treat in England, it bespoke some masterful scrounging.

In my drunkenness I boasted that my group was so accomplished that if I should order fried eggs from Primo he'd provide them. In fact, I said, he would serve fried eggs the length of the bar, far outshining the four that Bill had served me. Although most men had an "egg run" whereby they bartered cigarettes for eggs from nearby farmers, I had no evidence that Primo or anyone else on Grafton Underwood had that many raw eggs stashed away. It was an empty boast that I quickly regretted. But Bill saw his chance to insult me further and took me up on it.

"You're on," he challenged. "And I promise to eat 'em all."

"Okay. Primo!" I turned to the barkeeper. "Please provide General Gross fried eggs the length of the bar." I waved expansively.

"Yes, Sir, boss," Primo said with no other comment, and quickly disappeared.

"Take your time, Stooge," Bill said magnanimously.

I think we had both forgotten about the egg business when

Primo arrived with a large tray, upon which rested six warm plates, each one of which displayed two beautiful fried eggs. Ceremoniously he placed them down the length of the bar as Bill gaped.

"Stooge," he said humbly, "you've done it to me again. I guess this makes you the Maestro, Maestro."

"Yes, Stooge," I replied, "and now as a dutiful Stooge you got to eat all the eggs."

Bill fell to it with relish, but I hated to see all those precious eggs wasted, and I helped devour them along with Primo and others at the bar.

I happened to turn around and saw Bob Thacker frying eggs in the fireplace. He had overheard my stupid boast, had dug up his own cache of eggs, and was frying them in mess tins. He had no faith that Primo could pay off, and was doing his best to help me win the crazy bet. Then I noticed Oatis Parks, one of my squadron commanders, also attempting to save me from disgrace by frying eggs on top of a potbellied coke stove.

Next morning the cruddy sky and drizzle enhanced the throbbing of my head. Nevertheless the 384th was taking off on another mission to Germany. The thunder of hundreds of engines overhead, as the great formations assembled above the clouds, seemed to shake the world, but even with my headache the familiar thunder was music to my ears.

I gathered my gear together, said a few more good-byes, and let Bob Montgomery drive me one last time in the maroon Studebaker President to the railway station in Kettering. There I boarded a train to Prestwick, Scotland, where I would catch a C-54 to the States. Counting U-boat hunting days, my thirty-three months of combat had ended.

Ross Milton would send out many more missions before Hitler ended the war by committing suicide in his Berlin bunker. Like a dying animal he occasionally struck back viciously. From time to time the defeated Luftwaffe would be launched from well-camouflaged positions and take bloody bites out of Ross Milton's combat boxes, while the murderous flak never entirely let up.

And there would be another frigid winter to endure at 20,000 feet. Not until mid-April of 1945 did the 384th stand down. That was when General Spaatz announced that since there were no more strategic targets in Germany, the Combined Bomber Offensive was over.

Epilogue

Bursting with ideas, I landed in Washington with vain and inflated plans to reshape the conduct of the air war. I suppose front-line soldiers throughout history have always believed that the rear-echelon desk-borne soldiers know nothing about running a war, and the remote staff officers are perpetually screwing up the works, causing men to die needlessly.

But the Army Air Forces had a phenomenal leader, five-star general Henry "Hap" Arnold, who realized that his air troops were fighting a new kind of war that had only been conceived in the minds of a few great strategic thinkers. Hap Arnold, among them, knew that much of our air tactics and strategy was being played by ear. There was no score. And the proof of the new means of waging war was being gained in the contested skies around the world amid the shock of battle. Hap wanted staff officers in Washington who had been there and who had learned, catch as catch can, how to fight that kind of war.

I had no idea of the vastness of the new Pentagon or of the almost incomprehensible complexity of the bureaucracy that faced me. Full colonels were a dime a dozen and little more than peons in this maze that was aptly dubbed "the puzzle palace." I was too far down the ladder of rank to be greeted by Hap Arnold or even his deputy, and, as my orders directed, I checked in to the outer office of the director of Operations, Commitments, and Requirements. There I was given the title of Chief of Bombardment Requirements, and charged with the heady responsibility of establishing the requirements for bombardment aviation throughout the world. This meant the requirements for aircraft, personnel, and training. It also included the development of specifications for future bombers, a task that consumed much of my attention.

It didn't take me long to realize that there were a dozen other offices, many headed by generals, who were also involved with requirements. So to get anything done I had to coordinate my papers with them and convince them that my ideas were sound. At this task my combat service provided me with some authority.

My office consisted of about a dozen senior officers, all of whom had been handpicked for their smarts. Most had seen active service in various theaters of war and it was a pleasure to work with them. At least an equal number of comely secretaries added charm to the office. It took me some time to get used to working so closely to these lovely American girls, who compared with the dowdy British lasses like peacocks to chickens.

No more did I have to struggle with a coke stove. In the new Pentagon our offices were air-conditioned, with every convenient facility. But outside the Pentagon there was chaos. I stood in a long queue to ride an overcrowded bus, and invariably had to stand, with my head hitting the ceiling, for the hour's meandering trip to the room I had been lucky to find far out on Connecticut Avenue.

But before I reported to the Pentagon I had been granted an automatic month's leave provided to all those returning from a combat zone. Following this there was a mandatory debriefing and orientation period at Santa Ana in Southern California.

After landing in the States I headed straight for Reno in the nose of a B-25 going that way. My sister Jean was doing an outstanding job mothering Kort and Voan with the loving support of our parents. I did my best to spoil the kids, bringing them presents from Paris: a German helmet for Kort and a red dress from Schiaparelli's for Voan. It was a dream vacation, with no combat in the offing to spoil my relaxation, and I became much better acquainted with my kids. Things were going so smoothly that I decided not to disturb the family arrangement until after the war. Moreover, it would have been almost impossible for me to care for the two kids in crowded Washington where I knew I would be working long hours seven days a week.

Hitler, madman that he was, continued to wage war. His last-gasp offensive in the Ardennes resulting in the Battle of the Bulge was a tragic waste of life. Casualties ran into the seventy thousands on both sides. From time to time the Jerries would hoard enough gas to launch some of their new jet fighters. Our slower prop-driven fighters were almost helpless against them and now and then we would suffer cruel losses. Nevertheless our ultimate victory was assured. The whole German countryside was dying from starvation of fuel, and transportation was in a shambles. The armies of the western Allies and Russia were rapidly closing together, pinching the last life out of *der Reich*, while Hitler cowered in his Berlin bunker.

I regretted not having the opportunity to celebrate V-E day back at Grafton Underwood with my group. What ecstasy they must have enjoyed! But now our attention in the Pentagon turned entirely to the war in the Pacific. Curtis LeMay was pounding Japan with his B-29s and the Japanese empire was rocking on its heels.

Precision bombing of strategic targets had not proved particularly successful against Japan. Perhaps it would have succeeded eventually after tactics had been adjusted to fit the special conditions of that theater and the particular weaknesses of the Japanese economy. But Washington was anxious to win the war and the niceties, not to mention the morality, of the strategic bombing concept were not generally known or accepted in high circles. Gen. George C. Marshall, the Army chief of staff, had estimated that the invasion of Japan would cost us a million casualties. Everyone wished to avoid this, and hoped that Japan could be brought to her knees by the blockade and bombing offensive before the planned invasion.

Strategic bombing had been a phenomenal success over Germany. Philosophers throughout the ages have abhorred the violence and cruelty of war, and speculated on how a less lethal kind of war might be waged. Here was the answer. We could attack war resources, not people. We could deny to the enemy the wherewithal to wage war. Perhaps we could find the keystone of an enemy economy that when destroyed would bring down the whole edifice. Over Germany we had finally found that keystone: petroleum. We had come close to completely obliterating oil production and storage.

Another was her transportation system. A modern country would starve without the vast communications networks that feed it. But transportation was a much more difficult target system to destroy. Its interwoven and redundant lines covered the whole country and it was easier to repair them than, for example, the synthetic petroleum plants. Nevertheless, repeated attacks by the massive Allied strategic air forces, one raid of which was made with over four thousand bombers, crippled Germany's transportation system so that freight car loadings almost diminished to zero.

Early in the war American planners thought they had found an Achilles' heel in the German ball bearing industry and the Eighth took bloody losses at Schweinfurt where the principal plants were located. In fact our losses were so great that the whole concept of precision daylight bombing was threatened and we were urged by the RAF and even by many American leaders to abandon the concept and adopt the nighttime area bombing subscribed to by the British. However our air leaders stuck to their principles and weathered the storms of criticism.

Although our attacks against Germany's ball bearing production hurt German industry somewhat, we couldn't totally cut off the supply of bearings, many of which were purchased from neutral countries, such as Sweden. But the Reich had nowhere to go for more oil. General Eaker's Fifteenth Air Force in Italy kept pounding the Rumanian Ploesti oil fields into rubble and the Soviets had cut off the supply of oil from the east.

It became evident to the strategic planners that if precision bombing were to become a war-winning strategy it would be necessary to blockade the whole enemy country, permitting no imports of vital supplies. An island empire such as Japan was a good candidate for this kind of warfare, particularly when our Navy had gained almost uncontested command of the sea.

In Japan, industries were so dispersed and there was so much "cottage industry," that it was difficult to find significant strategic targets supporting key industries needed for Japan to wage war. Also, the B-29s, bombing from altitude, adopting the Eighth Air Force tactics learned over Europe, were too often missing their targets. A fierce jet stream over Japan slowed the formations so that they were subjected for long periods to flak and fighter attacks on the bomb run. When bombing downwind, the 200-mph wind took them across the target too fast to permit accurate bomb aiming. Unknown ballistic winds and turbulence below the B-29 bomb bays too often caused bombs to fall erratically. Additionally, the Wright engines of the B-29s were not quite powerful enough to take the strain of the heavy takeoffs and the battles against the jet headwind, and too many of the engines would burst into flame.

Because of the widespread cottage industries, Tokyo itself seemed to be a strategic target. Moreover the city was highly flammable, with many square miles of bamboo and wicker structures. The argument put forward by the Royal Air Force that area bombing of population centers would eventually destroy a nation's morale and cause it to capitulate, versus the strategic bombing concept of the Army Air Force, still raged. The direct evidence of the latter's success in Europe, as determined by the postwar Strategic Bombing Survey, was not in, and the area bombing of Dresden almost at war's end, by both the Royal Air Force Bomber Command and the Eighth Air Force, illustrated how pervasive was the RAF argument.

The indecisiveness of the high-altitude precision bombing over Japan, combined with the troubles caused by the under-powered B-29s, led Gen. Curtis LeMay and his superiors to shift the strategy to low-level area fire bombing. To gain better performance and reduce engine fires the big Superfortresses were stripped of guns and gunners.

Cruel as the fire bombing of Tokyo was, this tactic soon proved successful. Before many weeks, Japanese leaders were seeking avenues for negotiating a surrender. It might be noted here that there was little compassion for Japan in America. We still smarted from the surprise attack on Pearl Harbor, which President Roosevelt had called a "day of infamy," not to mention the cruelty of the death march from Bataan.

About this time the new atomic bomb became operational. This could be nothing else but an area weapon because of its wide lethal radius. The scientific community that had developed this so-called absolute weapon was eager to employ it, and President Harry Truman approved the go-ahead. The almost supernatural effect of the bombs dropped on Hiroshima and Nagasaki shocked the Japanese government into an immediate capitulation.

One might say that area bombing over Japan was a success, no matter how inhumane. But with the advent of nuclear weapons, and the growing knowledge of the massive devastation and loss of civilian lives caused by area bombing, a general revulsion of bombing per se gripped the general populace. The concept of strategic bombing, where accurate drops took out key industries with surgical precision, limiting the loss of life to a few factory workers, was little appreciated or accepted. Compared to modern surface warfare, where massive armies like deadly vacuum cleaners destroyed everything in their paths—farms, villages, cities, and people—strategic bombing was far less wantonly destructive.

Few air leaders suggested that strategic bombing could have won the war alone. Surface warfare in Europe, with Germany crushed between two massive ground offensives, bled the country white and bombing accentuated the hemorrhage. Perhaps the Reich would have capitulated by bombing alone, but had we not provided a second front we would have granted the Soviet Union a gift of all Europe. Political considerations demanded our invasion, whether or not airpower alone could have forced Germany to surrender.

In the Pacific, airpower was the decisive force that caused Japan to capitulate. The turning point in the war was the great victory at the Battle of Midway by carrier airpower. However, the heavy bomber offensive against the home islands couldn't have taken place without bases within striking distance of the Japanese targets. Surface forces provided these bases in the Marianas, while the U.S. Navy effectively destroyed Japan's seapower.

That isn't to say that airpower, used effectively, under favorable circumstances, couldn't win a war alone, just as armies and navies have won wars alone in the past. Portents of things to come were noted when bombing alone caused the island of Pantelleria in the Mediterranean to capitulate. And considering the global range and high performance of modern aircraft and munitions, there is less need today for advanced bases.

One thing that all the air leaders agreed upon, however, was that the Air Force was of equal importance in warfare to the Army and Navy, and that the Air Force should be a separate service on an equal basis with the surface forces. In this they had the support of Generals Marshall and Eisenhower, although there was some resistance from the admirals who wanted their own air force and had come to rely almost exclusively on the aircraft carrier as their capital ship.

Although some of these thoughts passed through my mind and were frequently the objects of discussion while I served the last six months of the war in the Pentagon, my immediate concerns involved providing better engines for the B-29s and better radar bombing equipment and stopping the manufacture of the B-32, which was demonstrably inferior to the B-29, of which we now had more than we could fly. This released thousands of people that we needed for our expanding B-29 groups, not to mention the multimillion-dollar savings involved. I went to mockups of new bombers proposed by the aircraft industry and reported on strengths and limitations. When the war ended most of these contracts were canceled, but I managed to convince Gen. Hoyt Vandenberg, then director of Operations, Commitments, and Requirements, that we should keep the huge intercontinental, six-pusher-engined B-36, and it became our main defense and deterrent while America disarmed with abandon. I was also involved in work to improve the training manuals and schools for training our combat crews, and even, from time to time, helping with operations such as the B-29 mining of the Shimonoseki Strait to halt the flow of coal to the main island of Honshū.

At last the yearned-for V-J day arrived, and the great war we had fought on two fronts to successful conclusions ended. America had hardly realized its almost unlimited strength until it engaged in World War II. Now, it seemed, we could do anything, such as bring lasting peace to the world through the United Nations. We even tried to internationalize the atomic bomb, but the USSR couldn't appreciate such enlightened diplomacy and refused to accept our magnanimous proposal. We could win the greatest war of history, but winning world peace seemed to be just beyond our grasp.

Nevertheless, some contend that nuclear airpower has deterred a war with the Soviet Union, although now much of the airpower resides in intercontinental nuclear missiles. No one doubts that these massive weapons could win or lose a war by themselves. Their awesome destructive force, however, might cause both sides to lose, and, because of this, in another war they might be sequestered by mutual consent. Then the concept of strategic bombing of key industrial targets might again become our policy.

For myself, I managed to get transferred to March Field in Southern California where I could raise my two children in an atmosphere of peace.

Appendix 1

Combat Reports of the Merseberg Mission

The following combat reports of the Merseburg mission described in chapter 17 were prepared after the last crew had been interrogated by Pop Dolan's Intelligence people. He had to borrow officers from the squadrons to have enough people to interview the forty-five crews who landed at Grafton Underwood. Each crew of ten sat around a separate table where shots of whiskey were provided by the medicos. This was to help the crewmen relax and tell their stories to the interrogating officer.

*My duty as the leader was to phone Wing and Division and give them a quick account of the mission. Then I told Pop Dolan what I remembered about the raid and headed for my quarters where I had my own shot of whiskey. Pop Dolan later sent me the following detailed reports, which I forwarded to Division.—*D.O.S.

HEADQUARTERS
AAF STATION 106

Office of the Intelligence Officer

APO 557
29 July, 1944

SUBJECT: Air Commander's Narrative, 41st Combat Bombardment Wing "B," on Mission flown 29 July, 1944.

TO: Commanding Officer, AAF Station No. 106, APO 557.

The following Narrative by Colonel DALE O. SMITH, Air Commander, 41st Combat Bombardment Wing "B," on Mission flown 29 July, 1944:

1. Ten (10) aircraft, plus two (2) PFF aircraft, took off between 0555 and 0603 hours to attack Synthetic Oil Plant at MERSEBURG, Germany. These aircraft formed the Lead Group of the 41st Combat Bombardment Wing "B".

   a. Number of aircraft taking off including spares: 10
      Number of A/C taking off less unused spares: 10
      Number of A/C attacking any target: 9
      Number of A/C not attacking: 1
      Number of A/C returning to base: 10
      Number of A/C unaccounted for: 0
      Number of A/C known missing: 0
      Number of sorties flown: 9

   b. A/C No. 7142, Lt. HAYES, pilot, turned back over the field because of low oil pressure. His 20 × 250 GP Bombs were brought back.

2. No aircraft of this Group are missing.

3. Assemblies of the Group, Wing and Division were very good. Group assembly was completed over Base at 0703 hours, altitude 16,000 feet. Wing assembly was effected over ELY at 0722 hours, altitude 16,200 feet. Division assembly was not exactly as briefed, due to multi-layered clouds. We departed the English Coast at LOUTH at 0745 hours, altitude 15,800 feet.

4. The route out was flown over 10/10ths clouds. All formations after entering enemy territory were very good. The 41st "B" Wing, which I commanded, flew very close and was almost an integral part of the 41st "A" Wing, since PFF equipment assigned to the 41st "B" Wing went out. Word of visual bombing conditions was received from the Scouting Force, but considerable difficulty was encountered in getting intervals, since the 41st "B" in flying so close to 41st "A", had closed up all the

intervals, and were rather closely jammed up. However, I decided to fly 1,000 feet above the briefed altitude in order to avoid prop wash on the bomb run. We reached the IP at 1005 hours, altitude, 26,000 feet, and continued on the bomb run at that altitude.

5. The bomb run was made perfectly. The Bombardier informs us that it was an excellent run in every respect. Bombs were away at 1019 hours from 26,000 feet on a Mag. Heading of 092 degrees. No strikes were visible because of the heavy smoked target. Flak at the target was moderate and accurate. Weather was CAVU [ceiling and visibility unlimited].

6. We made a sharp right turn off the target, and I was unable to find the 41st "A" Lead, as enemy fighters were active. I picked the first Wing I could find with PFF aircraft leading and joined it. My Low Group did likewise. My High Group joined another Wing with PFF aircraft and I advised them to remain in that formation. Route back was uneventful. Numerous fighters were encountered in the target area, although none directly attacked my Group formation to my knowledge.

7. Fighter escort was very effective, except in the target area, where apparently it was swamped.

8. This Mission was excellently planned and conducted. Had PFF equipment assigned to 41st "B" been operational there would have been no problems whatever.

W. E. DOLAN
Major, Air Corps
Station S-2 Officer

Note: Two PFF aircraft with radar bombing equipment were loaned to us from another station which specialized in blind bombing. This made a total of 12 aircraft in the lead air Group. Flying over a solid undercast on the route out required radar navigation which could only be accomplished with the loaned PFF aircraft. After their equipment went out, it was necessary for me to follow closely the air Wing ahead, 41 "A," to take advantage of their radar navigation. A similar problem occurred on the withdrawal leading me to seek formations with PFF *equipment.* —D.O.S.

The reports from my High and Low air Groups which made up the air Wing, 41 "B", of the 384th, follow. —D.O.S.

HEADQUARTERS
AAF STATION NO. 106

Office of the Intelligence Officer

APO 557

29 July, 1944

SUBJECT: Low Group Leader's Narrative, 41st Combat Bombardment Wing "B", on Mission flown 29 July, 1944.

TO: Commanding Officer, AAF Station No. 106, APO 557.

The following is Narrative by Major G. B. SAMMONS, Low Group Leader, 41st Combat Bombardment Wing "B", on Mission flown 29 July, 1944:

1. Twelve (12) aircraft, without spares, took off between 0603 and 0618 hours to attack Synthetic Oil Plant at MERSEBURG, Germany. These aircraft formed the Low Group of the 41st Combat Bombardment Wing "B".

a. Number of A/C taking off including spares:	12
Number of A/C taking off less unused spares:	12
Number of A/C attacking any target:	12
Number of A/C not attacking:	0
Number of A/C returning to Base:	12
Number of A/C unaccounted for:	0
Number of A/C known missing:	0
Number of sorties flown:	12

b. A/C No. 2459, Lt. SEIDLEIN, Pilot, landed at FOULSHAM, for an unknown reason. A/C No. 7224, Lt. TOLER, landed at HETHEL, due to battle damage. Neither of these crews have yet returned to this Base, but it has been learned that each of these aircraft dropped 20 × 250 GP Bombs on the primary target.

c. A/C No. 2617, Lt. PATELLA, Pilot, was forced to leave the formation due to failure of No. 1 engine. This aircraft dropped 20 × 250 GP Bombs on a target of opportunity near MINDEN, Germany.

2. No aircraft of the Low Group, 41st Combat Bombardment Wing "B" are missing.

3. Assembly of the Group was effected over the Base at 0705 hours, altitude 15,000 feet. Wing was assembled from Base to KIMBOLTON at 0714, altitude 15,000 feet. Division assembly was completed at 0806 hours, 53 deg. 07 min. N—01 deg. 14 min. E, altitude 16,000 feet. Nothing out of the ordinary occurred during assemblies except that action was taken to avoid cloud layers.

4. On the route out Point "C" could not be made good because of cloud layer. Division departed Point "B" and flew a roundabout route to Point "Q". We crossed the enemy coast at 0902 hours, 53 deg. 28 min. N—05 deg. 57 min. E, altitude 21,000 feet. No enemy aircraft were encountered enroute to the target, although several were observed attacking Groups after bombs away. We reached the IP at 1005 hours, altitude 25,000 feet.

5. At the target visibility was slightly restricted by haze and smoke screen. Flak at the target was intense and from inaccurate to accurate. Bombs were away 1019 hours from 25,000 feet on a Mag. heading of 095 deg., with unobserved results, although the TG reported intense black smoke coming from the target.

6. We made a right turn off the target. About five minutes after bombs were away the Group was attacked by FW 190s and at least one enemy aircraft was shot down, exploding in mid-air. Route back was essentially as briefed, although this Group joined two Groups of the 3rd Division, one of which dropped its

bombs on QUACKENBRUCK, following which the route back was flown as briefed. We departed the enemy coast at 1147 hours, 53 deg. 30 min. N—06 deg. 30 min. E, altitude 22,000 feet and recrossed the English Coast at 1312 hours at CROMER, altitude 1,000 feet. We landed at Base at 1355 hours.

7. Fighter escort was very effective.

8. In Division formation our Wing was too close to the Lead Wing, probably due to the fact that PFF equipment in two lead ships became inoperative.

W. E. DOLAN
Major, Air Corps
Station S-2 Officer

For some unknown reason the leader's name of the High Group was not mentioned in the next report.—D.O.S.

HEADQUARTERS
AAF STATION NO. 106

Office of the Intelligence Officer

APO 557
29 July, 1944

SUBJECT: High Group Leader's Narrative, 41st Combat Bombardment "B" on Mission flown 29 July, 1944.

TO: Commanding Officer, AAF Station No. 106, APO 557.

1. Thirteen (13) aircraft, including one (1) Spare, took off between 0545 and 0618 hours to attack Synthetic Oil Plant at MERSEBURG, Germany. These aircraft formed the High Group, 41st Combat Bombardment Wing "B".

a. Number of A/C taking off including spares: 13
   Number of A/C taking off less unused spares: 12
   Number of A/C attacking any target: 12
   Number of A/C not attacking: 0

Number of A/C returning to Base: 12
Number of A/C unaccounted for: 1
Number of A/C known missing: 1
Number of Sorties Flown: 12

b. A/C No. 24330, Lt. MARTIN, Pilot, turned back as briefed. His 20 × 250 GP Bombs were returned to Base.

2. One (1) aircraft of the High Group, 41st Combat Bombardment Wing "B", is missing.

a. A/C No. 7870, Lt. SWEENEY, Pilot, is missing. At 52 deg. 30 min. N.—08 deg. 20 min. E., after the target, this aircraft was heard calling for fighter support, although not observed leaving the formation. This aircraft dropped 20 × 250 GP Bombs on the Primary Target.

3. Assembly of the Group, which was good, was completed at 0705 hours over GRAFTON UNDERWOOD Buncher at 17,000 feet. Assembly of the Wing was completed normally at 0721 hours, altitude 16,500 feet. It was necessary to omit one control point on Division assembly due to weather difficulties, the Wing Air Commander acting upon instructions of the Division Air Commander. Division assembly was finally effected at 0745 hours at which point we departed the English Coast.

4. Route out was flown as briefed in good formation. We had no encounters with enemy aircraft enroute to the target. We crossed the enemy coast at 0902 hours, 53 deg. 24 min. N.—06 deg. 04 min. E., where we were engaged by meager flak. We reached the IP at 1005 hours, altitude 26,500 feet.

5. Visibility at the target was unrestricted, although the target was obscured by a dense smoke screen and smoke from previous bombings. Flak was intense and accurate. This Group flew the briefed route from the IP to the target and aimed on the briefed MPI. Bombs were away at 1021 hours from 26,500 feet on a Mag. Heading of 095 deg., with unobserved results. Dense smoke, presumably from oil fires, was observed at the target.

6. Immediately after bombs away this Group, going out of

the target area, was attacked by enemy fighter aircraft, notably ME 109s, which made one pass at this Group. This Group was unable to assemble with the Combat Wing Air Commander. We withdrew with the 379th Group which was short one Section. We advised the Combat Wing Air Commander of our position and he instructed us to remain where we were. We departed the enemy coast at 1159 hours, and recrossed the English Coast at 1307 hours, and landed at Base at 1352 hours.

7. Fighter escort was good on the route out. However, its effectiveness was doubtful, since the main enemy attack came in the target area and several B-17s were seen going down.

8. Suggest sending 18-ship Groups rather than 12-ship Groups on deep penetrations, since the fire power and defensive strength is thereby increased. If Groups were able to maintain Wing formation, this would not apply, but when Groups take interval to bomb targets individually, they are like "clay pigeons."

W. E. DOLAN
Major, Air Corps
Station S-2 Officer

Appendix 2

My Finest Moment

A Lead Bombardier's Mission to Peenemünde
By Col. Anthony Palazzo USAF (Ret.)

On the morning of July 18, 1944, I received the usual wake-up nudge and whisper, "Briefing at 0200 and breakfast 0345, Captain."

I was squadron bombardier of the 545th Bomb Squadron, 384th Bomb Group (H), 41st Combat Wing, 1st Air Division, Eighth Air Force. I was also a lead bombardier, who flew only when leading a group which was in turn leading a wing or division of B-17 aircraft. A group formation at the time consisted of eighteen to twenty-four aircraft, a wing consisted of three groups, and a division was made up of three or more wings.

The 384th Bomb Group, under command of Col. Dale O. Smith, was at that time enjoying the distinction of being one of the hottest groups in the Eighth Air Force. However, the recent missions flown by the group on the sixteenth and seventeenth of July over Munich and alternate targets turned out to be ineffective and far below our high standard. On the sixteenth, Munich was bombed on PFF (pathfinder) methods and the results were unobserved. On the seventeenth, the group deviated from Munich to try to destroy a bridge across the Oise Canal at Beautor, but the group failed to drop its bombs, due to some trouble with the interphone between the pilot and the bombardier. The group finally laid its bombs on the marshaling yards at Laon,

235

with poor results even though the weather was CAVU (ceiling and visibility unlimited).

The results of these two missions infuriated both Colonel Smith and the group bombardier, Joe W. Baggs. Not only were they angry at this performance, but they were afraid that the group was going into a "bombing slump." The problem had to be cleared up before the next mission field order came in to the group Operations blockhouse. Their solution came in the form of a recommendation for me to fly as group lead bombardier, even though ordinarily it would not be my turn to fly. My squadron was due to lead the group, rather than the wing, as was the normal sequence of operational flying schedule.

At 0200 I reported for the special briefing given to the lead and deputy lead navigators and bombardiers. It usually lasted anywhere from forty-five minutes to an hour. The bombardier had to memorize the target configuration and all facets of the approach route from Initial Point (IP) of the bombing run, including landmark references and check points. It was the practice in the 384th that before the bombardier was allowed to leave the special briefing room, he had to draw from memory the bombing run scenario from IP to "Bombs Away" and MPI (mean point of impact) on the blackboard.

That morning I learned that the target for the July 18 mission was Peenemünde. I was fascinated by the site I was to bomb. Peenemünde was located on a peninsula protruding into the Baltic Sea. A large white building identified the target. It was the home of the V-2 rockets, where some of Germany's top scientists worked and lived.

I left the special briefing room and went to the Officers' Mess for my fresh-egg breakfast. Colonel Smith invited me to sit at his table and he asked me what I thought of the mission and target. I responded, "Sir, this entire operation is a bombardier's dream, and I'll do the best I can to hit it." Colonel Smith was pleased to hear my comment and told me that he could not overly emphasize the importance of this target. It was crucial to the war effort that it be destroyed.

We went to the large briefing room where all the crews were assembled to be briefed on this day's mission. All the particulars concerning this mission were explained: target, fuel load, bomb load, altitude, formation, assembly, routes, rendezvous points, flak areas, frequencies, call signs, and weather. Colonel Smith gave a pep talk and again stressed the importance of hitting Peenemünde. He stated that a hot bombardier was leading this effort, and he was confident that the mission would be a success. This vote of confidence in me enhanced my determination even more.

I was the lead bombardier of the eighteen aircraft of the 384th Bomb Group forming the high group in the 41st "A" combat bomb wing. Maj. George H. Koehne was our group leader, and Lieutenant Rovero was the lead navigator. The wing lead and low groups were flown by the 379th and 303rd Bomb Groups. They constituted the other two-thirds of the 41st "A" combat wing.

The eighteen aircraft of the 384th took off between 0453 and 0506 hours and assembled over the base at 0550 hours at 9,000 feet. Wing assembly was accomplished at 0601 hours at 10,500 feet. All speeds and climbs were normal and the division departed the English coast at 0646 at 11,000 feet.

The route led out over the North Sea, across the Danish Peninsula, and east over the Baltic Sea with Norway and Sweden to our left. The weather degenerated rapidly to eight-tenths cloud cover. I used pilotage navigation all the way over the North and Baltic Seas. I turned on my Norden bombsight and set all the necessary data into it, including trail, actual time of fall based on the bombing altitude of 26,000 feet, true air speed, and type of bomb. Each aircraft carried ten 500-pound general purpose bombs. Through an opening in the clouds I was able to pinpoint my position. I knew exactly where the target lay, even though it was completely covered with clouds. I felt I was quite prepared to attack the target successfully, and continued my pre-IP chores.

We were approximately ten minutes from the IP when I received a call from the group leader. He had received a message from the wing commander, he said, informing both the high and low groups that the wing lead bombardier couldn't see the target because of cloud cover, and that the groups should close formation for a PFF bomb run on the secondary target. I was told to turn off my bombsight and go into a PFF mode. The PFF bombing method at that time was very inaccurate, to say the least, and its chief result was the plowing up of potato fields in the Fatherland.

I was stunned by this turn of events, and I refused to accept what I had heard. Colonel Smith had impressed upon me the importance of hitting Peenemünde and the effect it would have on the war effort. I couldn't get that out of my mind. That knowledge, plus my meticulous preparation for this operation, gave me the courage to stand up against this command. I told the group leader that I could see where the target area was, and that he should proceed to it as briefed, and that I could hit it. He responded to the effect that he was closing formation as instructed for a PFF bombing run, and that I should act accordingly. In desperation I answered, "O.K., I'll obey your direct order to turn off the sight and prepare for a PFF bomb run, but when we get back to base and I'm interrogated I will tell them that I could see and hit the target, but you ordered me not to."

In response to my outburst the group leader said he would go along with me for a visual bomb run on Peenemünde. However, he made it perfectly clear what would happen if I missed. I already had a good idea of what would happen, but I prepared for the IP approach. It was pretty eerie up there without the wing lead and the low groups, which had closed formation and gone off to the secondary target. At the IP we turned to a magnetic heading of 233 degrees, at an altitude of 26,000 feet. I could see the coast of Sweden off to our left as we turned south-southwest towards the Peenemünde peninsula. Eighteen American B-17s were now flying alone, deep within enemy territory. We had no fighter escort. We were all by ourselves.

I began my sighting operation on objects that I could see on the visible peninsula coastline. I synchronized my drift and course hair perfectly and then synchronized the lateral cross hair, controlling the ground speed and rate of closure. My plan was to synchronize the bombsight as perfectly as I could on a visible object and then to move the hairs to where I thought the target lay, through visual triangulation techniques. As I went through these sighting operations, I saw a massive cloud that was sitting over the target begin to move off to the right. It was as if a great hand were sweeping the cloud away so that I could see the target. There it sat, the white building I had studied in the special briefing! I had been confident that I could have hit it through the clouds, but when I saw the target my tension changed to the kind of fantastic excitement that comes once or twice in a lifetime. I knew we would succeed.

I moved the cross hairs onto the target, leveled the bubbles, pulled up the bomb release trigger and sat there watching the rate index register move towards the tangent of the dropping angle index. The latter index registered the point in space for the bomb release and would release the bombs at that point automatically through the trigger switch. I was perfectly synchronized and the cross hairs were frozen on my aiming point. I couldn't miss!

At 1012 hours the two indices met and the bombs fell. To preclude the possibility of a switch malfunction I hit the manual salvo lever to make sure the bombs were released. I called out over the interphone, "Bombs away!" All seventeen aircraft bombardiers and togglers salvoed their loads on me the instant they saw the first bomb fall from my bomb bay.

I followed the bombs visually from my seat until I couldn't see them anymore, and then I waited for a minute and some seconds until I saw the bombs begin to burst on the target. It was the most beautiful sight I had ever seen. My ball turret gunner also visually followed the bombs all the way to impact. He actually had the best view in the aircraft. He shouted over the interphone, "Captain Tony, you really clobbered it!" There was excitement throughout the aircraft as we made a steep turn off the target and headed for the sea.

When we were well on our way home the group leader called, "Tony, would you please come up to the flight deck and bring your mission folder with you?" I responded, "Yes, Sir" and climbed up to the flight deck. The mission flight folder contained a photograph of the target and he asked me to show him where the bombs hit. I drew a circle around the MPI that had been briefed to me, and with this I could see his eyes sparkle. He immediately called the radio operator and sent the following message back: "Primary target attacked, bombing results excellent!" Our group leader was one happy guy, and so was I and everyone else who participated in that mission.

We recrossed the English coast at about 1300 hours at 2,000 feet. At this time two or three of the aircraft that carried cameras aboard left the formation and headed directly for the base so that the film would be processed by the time the group arrived and landed. When we landed and parked in our dispersal area, the flight line seemed to be ablaze with excitement. Colonel Smith, Colonel Ben Lyon, Lt. Col. William Buck, Major Joe Baggs, and others were there to congratulate us. They had seen the photographs and the results were excellent! We had carried out our mission.

Even though I do not have a record of who all the crew members were that day other than Lt. Rovero, with whom I worked very closely in navigating to the IP, I am grateful to all the crew members for their outstanding airmanship for making the success of that mission possible. Each successful mission was the result of good teamwork as well as individual skill. My very special thanks to Major Koehne, who stuck his neck out with me and gave me the opportunity to carry out the mission.